I0762677

THIS IS RUNNING

THIS IS RUNNING

A CELEBRATION OF THE WORLD OF RUNNING, EXPLORING THE CULTURE, HISTORY, BRANDS, RACES AND PEOPLE BEHIND IT

RAZIQ RAUF

Contents

Banque de Savoie
DACIA
UTMB
MONT BLANC

INTRODUCTION

Running is a radical act. The person you are at the end of a run is different to the person that took that first step. First and foremost, taking the time to turn up for your body and mind is a purposeful moment of self-care, but as you run, you learn things about yourself, the people you're running with, and the places you're travelling through. The unique ways in which you engage with the world while running form the essence of running culture, and it's different for every single person.

'As every runner knows, running is about more than just putting one foot in front of the other. It's about our lifestyle and who we are.'

So said Joan Benoit Samuelson, who won the first women's Olympic marathon in 1984. (That's right, women haven't always been allowed to run marathons, but more about that later.) Samuelson's remark is about how running is more than just physical movement. It's about how after you fully embrace being a runner, you end up changing everything else in your life to fit around your running practice. How once you understand you're a runner, it's curtains for your other hobbies. You begin to shape your social calendar around your weekend long run. It might even end up being easier to get a new group of friends who also run. You look forward to your runs, so getting out of bed early starts to only be a chore, rather than an impossible task, because no lie-in is worth running in the midday sun for.

It's with the weather that you begin to understand your relationship with the outdoors. Heat, cold or rain, you learn to adjust your routines accordingly. You start to understand why others may have adjusted theirs. Whether you're running alone or with a thousand people, you learn about your own body's limits. Maybe it's during the closed streets of a race day, or running through a public thoroughfare, but how you feel during either will change you. You're moving through the world at speed, relying only on your body's ability to propel you forward, and it's a beautiful thing, whether your doctor suggested that you try running for your weight or for your mental health, or if you were spurred to do it by something deep inside. Even though it's just running – the most immediately primal act for any child – you'll spend every moment doing something new.

We also engage with the sport in so many other ways – both tangible and not. There's running to look good, and there's running to feel good. You can run with every one of the latest gadgets adorning your person from head to toe, or you can run free, with only the wind in your ears. There's that focus on a training regimen designed by a coach, and there's running every Tuesday evening with your local community, whether you're trying to lead the pack, or hanging back to chat with friends both old or new. These are all the social and political ways in which we take part in the world of running.

How we grow up can help define our paths in so many weird and wonderful ways, but the goal is always contentment, if not happiness. There are stereotypical ideals associated with either Western or Eastern cultures, for instance, where individual versus collective success are valued differently, or focused upon at different moments, or indeed whether happiness is something to be sought after at all. While the somewhat hedonistic pursuit of happiness is deeply ingrained into everything that we do, everyone's idea of happiness and contentment is completely different, and how each of us achieves that is as well. Once we've paid our bills, and fed ourselves and our loved ones, every morsel of spare time and income is spent on something that we find worthwhile. We buy the ice cream, or donate to a local charity. We buy a ticket to see a movie, or we play a board game with a loved one. We go on a fairground ride, or plant some vegetables. We go for a run. We read a book.

After that broad definition of culture, with which I'm hoping to frame the many strands of running culture that we will look at throughout this book, let's think, for a moment, about how reading can be as radical an act as running. As you leaf through the pages of a book, you take on new information, perspectives and ideas that challenge and merge with your thoughts, changing your outlook on the world forever. The person you are at the end of a book is different to the person that first picked it up. Reading is just as monumental an act of self-love as running.

帝京大学
SAPPORO
30
SAPPORO
15
SAPPORO
141
上武大学
日本大学

A GLOBAL CULTURE

There is so much of this world to explore, so what better way to learn about different cultures than via running? Doesn't traversing the globe and seeing how every runner engages with their environment in a beautifully unique fashion sound like the perfect way to learn about the world?

What country, for instance, has a third of the population watching a long-distance relay race on television every January, while companies are closed for the New Year? That's Japan, where families come together to tune in *en masse* every year to watch 200 of the country's brightest students race 135 miles (217km) on foot from Tokyo and back again, passing a sash between themselves, rather than a baton, over two days in the Hakone Ekiden. With its origins in the country's ancient couriers, the race has central tenets of togetherness and community, and is a huge showcase event for young Japanese athletes.

Elsewhere in Japan, you might find a thousand-day pilgrimage by the Marathon Monks of Mount Hiei. *Kaihōgyō* is considered one of the most demanding challenges in the world, and is a search for enlightenment for these men who carry religious texts for dozens of miles across the mountains while wearing straw sandals. They engage in other spiritual activities like meditation, calligraphy and fasting over the three-year period. They also carry a knife and rope with them: is there another event dramatic enough to invoke the symbolism of ritual suicide in case of failure?

If you can't travel to those places yourself, you can travel using someone else's eyes, through the experiences that they've written about. Learn about the secrets of the African marathoners in *Running with the Kenyans* after Adharanand Finn lived with them for six months, or discover the Rarámuri - another group that runs in outrageously low-tech footwear - in Christopher McDougall's *Born to Run*. These brilliant writers immerse themselves in their subjects so intensely that they can't fail to come away with amazing stories.

OPPOSITE

Runners in the 89th
Tokyo-Hakone Collegiate Ekiden.

As we learn about the world, we start to notice inequities – both global and local – manifesting through running. The most surface-level thinking helps us understand how different climates affect our running. If you live in a warm, sunny place with low humidity, you might never even need to think about wearing a pair of gloves while running, let alone other cold-weather layers. That is a certain level of privilege that can easily be glossed over, but then consider how air pollution can factor into a running schedule. Living in a rural area, free of industry and heavy traffic, the issue of poor air quality may never need to cross your mind, but for runners in places like Mexico City or Lahore in Pakistan – the most polluted city in the world – the healthy act of running can turn a sharp corner to being a surefire way to develop asthma. The features of our immediate vicinity can be limiting in ways incomprehensible to others.

And what of Smog City, AKA Los Angeles? My adopted home is a major cultural epicentre, but flies somewhat under the radar in terms of running today. There is some hefty pedigree, with Santa Monica Track Club training the likes of nine-time Olympic gold medallist Carl Lewis, and Nike being founded in Santa Monica in 1966 as Blue Ribbon Sports, but despite those huge claims, it's New York that gets spoken about in terms of run clubs. And while the Los Angeles Marathon isn't close to becoming one of the major marathons, it is still a destination race because it passes through the bright lights of Hollywood.

In a car-oriented city where public transportation is sneered at by the moneyed masses inhabiting that star-studded central strip between Pasadena and Malibu, purposeful exercise is required to balance out the LA lifestyle that is so sedentary we can move between bed, car seat and desk chair, and back again, maybe via the sofa or a restaurant seat of your choice, without taking any meaningful steps that day. When hiking or yoga don't quite cut it, running the pavements is the way.

OPPOSITE

A Rarámuri woman running through Los Angeles in 2024.

Ante
Berlin
Ante

As running grows in popularity, more subcultures are added, and one of the options available to Angelenos is running under the influence of marijuana. It's an extension of the philosophy that brings people to beer miles (chugging 12oz (350ml) of light beer every quarter-mile), but with cannabis products. There is an increasing amount of science that points towards the anti-inflammatory properties of the drug, as well as the blissful benefits CBD has on one's mindset, but while it's freely available in California, and 23 other US states, running under the influence of cannabis is not an activity in which you can legally partake in the majority of the United States, let alone further afield.

This brings us to the question of who is free to run. Who truly has access to the sport, and how? We like to think that we are all free to act as we wish (within the law) in a civilized society, but that wasn't true in the tragic case of Ahmaud Arbery, who was chased down, shot and killed while running in Brunswick, Georgia. It was a sobering reality check for those who desperately want to believe that running has been completely normalized in supposedly developed nations. It should be unthinkable that you cannot run safely, but a Black man running was still able to highlight the unsavoury underbelly of modern life enough to ignite a fire underneath the Black Lives Matter movement, which is widely credited with forcing significant policy changes in the USA, such as bans on chokeholds by the police, as well as increasing efforts to end mass incarceration and systemic biases.

Would Arbery have faced the same problem if he had been running in the mountains? There are other dangers associated with trail running, of course (bears, snakes, precipitous drops), but you might be free of human judgement, at least. What if there isn't easy access to the trails from where you live, though? What if you don't have the time or money for a three-hour jaunt through the forest? What if the only option of outside you have available to you is mostly concrete?

A perfect example of exploration by running through concrete conurbations is how modern urban run crews come together around the world through their Bridge The Gap initiative. While their lived experiences of running overlap significantly, just by virtue of having so many similarities between the major cities in which they live, there are still intricate details that they share between one another. It could be something simple in terms of how they communicate, or how they celebrate, but by converging in one location and learning one another's patterns, new cultures are formed.

When anti-Chinese sentiment descended upon the world with the advent of the pandemic, there was a 361 per cent increase in anti-Asian hate crimes, so Chinatown Runners was formed in 2021 to bring runners from all over New York to Chinese neighbourhoods across the city in a new social-run experience. Part of the plan was to support local Chinese-owned businesses after they lost all their income overnight in 2020, and had not yet recovered, but part of the exercise was to help to bring people from adjacent neighbourhoods that were otherwise totally disconnected from each other's cultures.

This kind of activism is a huge reason why this current running boom has captured the attention of the younger generations. Running is a radical act, after all.

A NOTE ON MEASUREMENTS:

Some races around the world are measured in miles, some in kilometres, so sometimes distances in the book will be given miles first, sometimes kilometres (with conversions in brackets). To avoid too much of this, conversions of common race distances are given below and not in the book itself:

100 MILES = 161 KILOMETRES
26.2 MILES = 42.165 KILOMETRES (STANDARD MARATHON DISTANCE)
100 METRES = 109.4 YARDS
5 KILOMETRES = 3.1 MILES

Yuki Kawauchi

Winner of the 2018 Boston Marathon

Ekiden runner Kawauchi won the Boston Marathon in 2018 in dramatic fashion, powering through the cold wind and rain to take the lead over defending champion Geoffrey Kirui at mile 25. Interestingly, he wasn't a full-time professional athlete at the time, as he had a government job in a high school in the outskirts of his hometown of Tokyo, Japan.

TELL ME ABOUT YOUR EXPERIENCE RUNNING EKIDEN

I ran my first ekiden when I was 11 years old. I felt the joy and fulfillment of achieving a goal with my friends. In junior high school, I was captain of the ekiden club. I chose a high school where ekiden were popular, and practiced rigorously for ekiden rather than individual races. I chose my university based on my studies rather than ekiden.

WHAT MAKES THE EKIDEN A UNIQUE RACE FORMAT?

Even if a team loses to its other runners in the section ranking, it can still win the overall team ranking thanks to the other team members, and conversely, even if the team's overall ranking is poor, it can still be recognized with a 'section award'. There are no 'section awards' in track relays.

WHAT DOES EKIDEN MEAN TO THE JAPANESE PEOPLE?

In one word, I think it's 'bonds'. This includes friends, family, school, and community. I also think that the concepts of 'running,' 'working together to achieve a goal as a team', and 'school sports' were accepted by many Japanese people.

HOW IMPORTANT IS EKIDEN TO UNIVERSITY ATHLETES?

Some runners believe that there is no greater race than the Hakone Ekiden. Long-distance runners have known about the Hakone Ekiden since childhood, and they believe it is a race worth dedicating their life to because of the amount of attention it attracts. Also, participating in the Hakone Ekiden has an impact that brings happiness not only to your family, but also to your hometown and those involved.

WHAT IS POST-COLLEGIATE RUNNING LIKE IN JAPAN?

In the past, it was common for corporate teams to focus on the New Year Ekiden and then aim for marathons and track races. However, there are now runners like me, 'citizen runners' (former amateur runners), who are working full-time jobs and surpassing their student records in marathons and track races. I think there are more options for continuing to compete after graduating from university now than there were 16 years ago when I graduated.

WE RUN

Whether we run for necessity, joy or discovery, we run. And we've always run. It's human instinct; an age-old impulse. Survival. Evolution. Competition. It's all fundamental human behaviour with roots in deep evolutionary past that compels us to push our bodies into motion.

Even if running to hunt is now largely confined to a few native hunter-gatherer tribes dotted around the planet, the human body remains uniquely built for running long distances. Our notably long legs are attached to a skeletal structure that has adapted its gait and makeup of its musculature over time to help us run, even to the point that we have developed a specific ligament to stabilize our large heads. Our cardiovascular system has developed to carry more blood around the body, taking oxygen to our extremities more efficiently, and helping to thermoregulate our bodies via the evaporation of sweat. We're the only animal to have our own built-in cooling system. Genetically and ancestrally, we are running machines.

The need to run for survival has moved on from flexing superior stamina over a lion to a reaction to unfavourable blood panels resulting from the newly sedentary lifestyle that multiple industrial revolutions have foisted upon us. That running is one of the most highly recommended solutions to the increased prevalence of illnesses that come attached to our 21st-century lives is simply more evidence that human beings are born to run.

Take the example of our brains becoming active during this exertion. The endocannabinoid system starts producing cannabis-like compounds that regulate pain, mood and appetite, enhancing motivation and endurance as a glorious byproduct of this natural mind–body connection. Even if the exact biochemistry is not fully understood by the runner, the sensation of the 'runner's high' can become addictive – one that is as compelling as it is fulfilling.

Now, without the flight part of the fight-or-flight impulse charging our running, we are making choices to run. For competition, for friendship, for health. They are all compelling reasons to run, especially when those mental benefits are considered. The freedom that you feel as you course through nature is a stress reliever, and as the act of running becomes less difficult, you are encouraged by your more able body, and you set new goals. Those goals can ratchet up and up. Running begets more running. Movement becomes joy. Running becomes a primal urge again, but you're not being chased by a lion any more.

The impulse has transformed to deep purpose, and that sits comfortably with our desire for progress as a civilization, doesn't it? Unshackled by either hunting game or being hunted, it has a new perspective. There are records to be broken, charities to raise money for, issues to raise awareness about, personal health objectives. Despite running being an inherent part of our beings, now it is a choice, and – more often than not – it is a positive one that is thankfully borne far less out of fear for our lives. The reasons to run now are vast, but more than ever, they are now firmly rooted in desire rather than necessity.

The way you run now is the same as everyone who came before you who ran. While the physical act itself has remained largely unchanged over time – simply augmented by various strands of science – the ways in which we've run, the reasons, the methods, and how we come to the sport are deeply personal. When, why, where and how we run is unique to every runner, but however you run, it's always just you, and it always has been. So go and run.

When We Run

OUR FIRST RUN

Do you remember your first run? I'm not talking about the first time you ever ran. That would've happened moments after your very first toddling steps, because it's in our nature to run. I'm talking about the first time you left your home with the sole purpose of going for a run. Maybe it was in adulthood, and it was more difficult than you expected it to be. You were hoping to reclaim that feeling of freedom that you remember from running through the school playground, but your legs were heavier and your lungs more restrictive. For some, that initial disappointment is enough to put them off running again forever, but for those who persevere, it can become an all-consuming habit. Either way, what a commitment that first step was, whether it was out of your front door or onto a treadmill. That was the moment you conquered a new frontier in your mind. That was the moment that you became a runner.

AS A CHILD

About that playground experience. Whether it's during your school break or in the park with friends, running is a central part of childhood. With rules meted out left, right and centre by our parents about where we can go, how far we can go, and who we can go to those as-yet-unspecified places with, we took it to the limits (and maybe a little further), but time was always of the essence. Young minds are filled with the desire to explore, so quickly does it.

It's also likely that your first formal experience of running was at school. It's where you would have run your first 100-metre dash, and tried out for the athletics team. School is also where you may have been handed an unreasonable amount of laps to run as a punishment. That's not a way of instilling a healthy lifelong habit into a child, but maybe, like me, you joined the cross-country or athletics team because you weren't quite good enough for the football team, and the hard work that you undertook, stride after stride, has ending up resonating long into adulthood. That running in our formative years lives with us forever.

YOUR DAILY RUN

You run every day. It's your routine. Daily movement is an important part of the goal of a long, healthy life, so why not running? All you have to do is pull on a pair of running shoes and head out of the door. It's much less hassle than going to the pool or getting the bike out of the shed. Maybe you've worked your daily run into a run streak, or maybe you think about running the same way that you think about brushing your teeth – it's just something you do.

Either way, the physical and mental benefits of running as a ritual are clear. Running helps you sleep better, and it helps you clear your mind, which is nothing new. The Latin phrase *solvitur ambulando* means 'it is solved by walking'. Is the phrase about a mysterious mind–body connection, or simply outlining a practical solution to a complex problem? That's up to you: the runner.

IT'S RACE DAY

This is everything you've been training for. You know you're ready because you followed the plan your coach made for you, and you laid out your kit and nutrition last night and posted a photo of your flat lay. All those dozens, hundreds of miles have led to this. You're so goal-oriented that there is a clear distinction in your mind between those training runs and today. It's all about today. You ate your usual pre-race breakfast, and got to the race in plenty of time. You're in the lead corral, in the pack with the fastest runners, closest to the start line, so there won't be too much human traffic. You know what pace you need to run at, and you're going to hit your goal time. You visualize that finisher's medal being placed around your neck moments after crossing that finish line, and you begin to feel the nerves for the first time. The starter's gun goes off.

Why We Run

HEALTH IS EVERYTHING

Even running for five minutes a day can bring untold health benefits, like a reduced risk of early death, which is quite a big one. You might be running to improve your cardiovascular health, mental health, weight management or something else, like bone health or boosting your immune system, but you will simultaneously reap the benefits in so many other areas as well. For instance, if you're training for a marathon with a two-hour zone-two training run, where you're keeping your heart rate in the low-intensity steady-state popularized by author and coach, Matt Fitzgerald in his 2014 book, *80/20 Running, and* you run with a group, you can add a mental-health-boosting social element. Running can do so much for your well-being. You just have to do it.

PLEASURE THROUGH PAIN

While many will say that running for pleasure is the antithesis to running for performance, there is pleasure to be gained from achieving one's goals - for instance, the joy of a successful track session that you know will deliver benefits on race day - but when it's distinct from goals, running for pleasure can be a game-changer. Improving your health can be a part of the happiness gleaned from running, but it's a focus on pleasure in the moment that can really have an effect. The 'runner's high' is a complex release of hormones (endorphins, dopamine, endocannabinoids) created by the body that can quell pain or discomfort in favour of euphoria. That sensation can lead into the meditative flow state, where deep thinking can occur alongside the calming rhythmic cadence of your feet. Yes, it sounds like free drugs, and because the only payment is a few miles of running, it can be the thing that keeps many runners lacing up their shoes. Remember: pain is inevitable, but suffering is optional.

OPPOSITE

Race participants experiencing the 'runner's high'.

BANDIT
24
NEW YORK

RELEAS
tcs
TATA
CONSULTANCY
SERVICES
TATA

FINDING YOURSELF

Setting goals and working towards them is a fundamental aspect of human nature's desire for improvement and achievement. It's why the marathon is a bucket list event – it's an incredibly difficult feat to achieve and requires months of training both your body and mind. Crossing that finish line after 26.2 miles is huge. In the process of preparing yourself to complete the race, you've proven to yourself and to anyone who's paying attention that you are capable of following and executing a plan. The intense solitude of that training, even when among others, will have allowed for introspection and a quiet but constant acknowledgement of your abilities, and every physical and mental challenge that you overcome teaches you a lesson about yourself that you can take and use in other parts of your life. In the eternal search to understand ourselves, the power of the human spirit reigns supreme.

EXPLORE YOUR CITY

When I moved to Los Angeles, I decided I would explore my new home by running it. I started by signing up to races in as many different parts of this enormous city as possible, and then started my search for a run club that fitted as many of my criteria as possible. Through that casual but purposeful tourism, I now know LA like the back of my hand – both the good bits and the bad – and it all came through running the streets. In such a car-centric city, this knowledge has been invaluable, even when sitting in traffic.

Exploring a city you've travelled to is another kettle of fish, though. Once you've set your suitcase down in your hotel room, pulling on your running shoes and exploring this foreign, exciting locale that you've landed in is a great way to start a trip. If you've travelled with others, you'll be the one they turn to when they're wondering where the nearest coffee shop is. You'll likely be able to reel off a few, including the one that's probably the best, judging by the long line out of the door. There's no better way to understand the beautifully complex relationships between a place and its people than on foot, and how better than at speed?

OPPOSITE

Tommie Runz participating in a marathon.

Where We Run

IN THE CITY

Maybe it's because they're morning miles near your home that you're doing to get them over with for the day, or because urban scenery is more of a monotonous grey haze than scenic, but roads can often struggle to inspire. While the reliability of a concrete jungle (assuming no trees have taken it upon themselves to crack the pavement with their roots) can provide a wonderful clean slate for a runner to experiment with their workouts, the thrill of the open road somehow doesn't quite apply to running. While car-free streets during a marathon are a road runner's dream, there can be a certain drudgery associated with miles undertaken on asphalt. Regardless, we persevere, because these miles aren't going to run themselves.

ESCAPE TO THE COUNTRYSIDE

It's no accident that green is the internationally recognized colour for mental health awareness. Green is the colour most associated with being outdoors; and nature, with its tweeting birds and warm sunshine, can be a beautifully calming experience. Green shoots, that you may have grown yourself, are also linked to symbols of growth and hope, which are strong themes in mental health recovery. When mental health conditions are estimated to cost the global economy $1.6 trillion per year globally, maybe more time spent in green spaces is wise. All that means that running in nature is a wonderful way to live life.

OPPOSITE

Trail runners descend the slopes.

ON THE HAMSTER WHEEL

Lovingly nicknamed the Dreadmill or the Shredmill, depending on whether the person lives with their glass half empty or half full, this piece of gym equipment is very reasonably likened to a hamster wheel, and we're better than hamsters, aren't we? While treadmills can provide a level of consistency, accessibility and shelter from the weather, stints on the treadmill are most often spoken about as monotonous running for running's sake. During times of poor air quality, though, the treadmill can offer that place to get your miles in even when everything might literally be on fire. Maybe it's worth learning to love the treadmill.

TRACK NIGHT

While this is where we find out who the fastest human on the planet is every four years at the Olympic Games, when was the last time you tested out how fast you can go? The freedom of flying down a track as fast as you can, with no distractions, straining every sinew in a bid to shave milliseconds off your time, is difficult to replicate elsewhere, and yet it's far less common for adults to take to the track. Going back to that 80/20 workout principle, while 80 per cent of our training should be in zone two, the other 20 per cent of your running should be a high-octane workout, and getting a sweat on at the track certainly fits the bill.

OPPOSITE

Runners at track night.

How We Run

ALL ON YOUR OWN

The loneliness of the long-distance runner has been pondered for some time, but circumstance often dictates that we run alone. Whether it's due to flexibility of our schedules versus the more rigid scheduling of team sports, the desire to run at a specific pace as part of a training regimen, or simply to have some peace and quiet for a moment to think during some alone time, running solo is a popular pursuit. In terms of self-improvement mentally, one of the key benefits to running alone is being able to gauge and improve your motivation levels, because the only person on the hook for you going on the run is you. All you have to do is lace up your shoes and take that first step out of the door. Easy, right? Keep telling yourself that.

FIND YOUR RUN CLUB

From school athletics and university cross-country teams to the local running store events, urban run crews, and the spate of corporate running-related activities that have been flooding Strava in increasing numbers, running groups have existed for centuries, in many different formats. In their purest form, run clubs are a place of solace where you can convene with your peers and measure your hard work. The idea of community is different for everybody, but there's definitely something out there for you. Maybe there will be some freebies at the end. Maybe it'll just be friendship.

OPPOSITE

A solo runner taking on 50km (31 miles) between Altadena and the Pacific Palisades in Los Angeles runs past the Arclight Dome, Hollywood.

CINERAMA

29
HORIO
30
KAWAI
6
LEMI
24
118
106
25
MURAYAMA
27
SONODA
105
26
SATO
119
MHPS
104
109
101
MHPS
169
156
113
112
129
140
126
146
161
218
SUZUKI
159
102
120
155
JFE
186
170
142
JFE
153
160
162

FIND A RUNNING PARTNER

Finding a regular running partner is one of the holy grails of running. It might be someone that you meet at an organized running club, or someone you met online through a classified ad (yes, this happens), but the search for that special someone is long and arduous. When you find that person who lives nearby, runs at a similar pace to you, has a similar world view and interests to you, and might even want to train for races together, hold on to them tight. You can go on adventures of self-discovery together, book trips to faraway places and save on the hotel room, and have some real, unavoidable accountability when you have to wake up at 5am for your long run.

I AM SPEED

Laymen and beginners alike see running a marathon as the main event of road running. You may have grown up hearing about the running of a marathon as a once-in-a-lifetime race, but with the platforming of the seven marathon majors (which is expanding to eight and then nine races around the world, dependent on qualification), the new challenge is to run all of the major marathons in one calendar year. Running multiple marathons in a year is difficult enough even without considering winning a bib in the lotteries or achieving qualification times, as well as the expense of travel, and the time off work. Has the marathon become a normal distance?

OPPOSITE

Runners competing in the Tokyo Marathon.

ESSENTIAL RACES

It's easy for the seasoned runner to forget how difficult that first run is, but to the non-runner, anyone running a race of any distance is a superhuman, and the marathon is the race that's most deeply embedded in the public's psyche. Whether you're running 5km or 26.2 miles, to them, you're running a marathon.

For most people, running a marathon is a serious undertaking. The training for a full marathon becomes an all-encompassing activity. You have to ramp your weekly distance up so your time spent running each week resembles a full shift at work, and because of all the extra exercise, you have to eat so much more food. Marathoning is both expensive and time-consuming.

In 2006, however, marathoning became even more expensive and time-consuming when the World Marathon Majors was formed. Bringing together Boston, London, Berlin, Chicago and New York marathons, with Tokyo joining in 2013 and Sydney in 2025, the championship-style format brought a new incentive to the competitive nature of runners. Gotta collect 'em all!

Building a reward-based goal around collecting tokens from challenges all over the world might seem like the basis of a smash hit video game, and the Marathon Majors are a similarly golden ticket to success. Of course there's a special six- ... sorry, seven-star finisher's medal for those who successfully incorporate the joys of taking run-cations to the biggest and best marathons around the world with a life of gruelling, extensive endurance training. Having a 26.2 sticker on the back of one's car used to be enough, but cut to 2025 and the ability to write '7* finisher' in your Instagram bio is the new mark of a serious (and affluent) marathoner.

With Shanghai and Cape Town marathons entering the multi-year candidacy process to join the cohort, the challenge to complete all majors in one calendar year could become one for the elites only. There is a world beyond those nine marathons, of course.

With well over 50,000 running the Paris Marathon and 30,000 running the Amsterdam and Mexico City marathons, there are enormous marathons elsewhere in the world. An issue with these big city races, however, is that you might not get a hotel room very close to the start line, and that's only if you successfully navigate the lottery system that's in place for so many of them. This means you might need to wake up four hours before the race start time to travel into the centre of Paris. It's unlikely you would've had a good night's sleep, and because you'll likely be hungry again by the time you start running, you might have to add in another layer of training so you can manage your nutrition.

There are good alternatives for marathons where the race might mirror your training and preparation a little more closely, and they often have some additional benefits. If either running under the canopy of historic, towering Redwood trees found in *Star Wars* and *Jurassic Park*, or along the iconic, scenic Californian coastline highway that Jack Kerouac took road trips along appeals to you, consider The Avenue of the Giants Marathon or Big Sur Marathon as perfect destination races.

Those are just two fantastic American races in my home state, and while a smaller race might save you time in terms of both getting to the start line and how many bodies you have to dodge, with fewer people, you're also less likely to encounter the rabid cheer zones that line the streets of London and New York. That extra bit of encouragement that you might get from someone screaming your name as you push through in Limehouse might only be there at the finish line in Poughkeepsie.

With a whole world of thoughtfully created races out there with varying difficulty and atmospheres to explore, you can find your perfect race day experience, and add another layer of mystique to your superhuman marathoning.

The London Marathon

Founded in 1981, the prestige and carnival atmosphere of the London Marathon has long attracted runners from all over the world, and with 56,640 finishers in 2025 it officially became the largest marathon in the world. Over 1.1 million people applied to run the 2026 edition, and while there are only 20,000 ballot entries available, there is another way to get a bib: raising money for charity. While the London Marathon is an important race both in sporting terms and for the wider running community, undoubtedly the most important part of the event is how much money its participants raise for charity. The London Marathon is the world's largest annual single-day fundraising event, with over £75 million raised at the 2025 event alone, and over £1 billion raised since its inception.

OPPOSITE

Runners competing in the London Marathon.

TravellingFit
FENO
57114
MAGGIE
66811
33294
sense
70 years
CLARE
36075

The Boston Marathon

If you're looking for the gold standard of road racing, look no further than the Boston Marathon. It's the world's oldest marathon, and is notoriously difficult to get a bib for. The prestige and difficulty of running Boston means that it's increasingly the prime target of the serious amateur runner. Similar to hanging a six-star medal around one's neck, achieving a Boston qualifying time is a serious flex. Not only do you have to run a marathon with a qualifying time at a qualifying event just to enter the ballot, but only two-thirds of ballot entrants get the opportunity to run up Heartbreak Hill – the culmination of all your efforts, near the end of 4 miles (6.4km) of undulating hills on an incredibly challenging course, it's the final climb, and it's at mile 20 – where you might hit The Wall.

Heartbreak Hill was named in 1936, when defending champion Johnny Kelley gave Indigenous runner Ellison Brown a pat on the back while passing him on this portion of the Newton hills. Brown, nicknamed Tarzan, was incensed and sprinted past Kelley on the hill, ultimately taking the first of his two Boston Marathon wins.

OPPOSITE

Ellison Brown crosses the finish line.

PROVIDENCE
TERCENTENARY
147
FINISH

DRIVE
CAREFULLY
Come Back
SOON
YESCO

The Speed Project

It's the most exclusive relay race in the world, and it's also the most gruelling: 340 miles (547km) of unsanctioned, unsupported racing across unforgiving desert and highway between the bright lights of Los Angeles and Las Vegas, this is The Speed Project (TSP). It has fast become the coolest, most Instagram-friendly running event on the calendar. It was a new breed of race for a new generation of runner. Likened to the running world's equivalent of Burning Man festival, TSP attracts renegade runners and those who want to get as close to breaking the rules as possible, even if there are no rules. Maybe it's honour among thieves, but the event fosters incredible community as well.

The route, between the two most vulgar bastions of American excess, is completely unguided and unmarshalled up to the individual teams to navigate. Consequently, the distance travelled through the Mojave Desert and Death Valley by different teams can vary by dozens of miles, but they all have 48 hours to complete the journey. That means that the support crew and the runners are in it together as they traverse some of the most barren terrain in the American West. Running through those stark landscapes looks wonderful on film, of course, so expect every type of visual documentation.

OPPOSITE

A team of runners celebrates at the finish point of The Speed Project.

Barcelona '92
695
USA
Barcelona '92
1738

Olympic 100m

It's unlikely that anyone reading this book will have taken part in this race, but there's a very high likelihood that everyone has watched the Olympic 100m sprint, at least on television. There's only one place to find the fastest man or woman in the world, after all. As one of the blue-ribbon events of the games, its brilliant simplicity makes it one of the highest-profile events. In this world of reducing attention spans, anyone, anywhere in the world, can watch and understand exactly what's happening between the starting gun and the finish line. The men's 100m record has fallen seven times at the Olympic Games. Usain Bolt made it his own most recently, in London in 2012, but you can go back 100 years to see athletes squeezing out every last drop of performance out of their body. They want to win, and they have less than 10 seconds to do it.

OPPOSITE

Linford Christie winning the 1992 Olympic 100m gold medal.

UTMB

The Ultra-Trail du Mont Blanc, which starts and ends in Chamonix, France, with a route that also travels through the Swiss and Italian Alps, is seen by many as the snowy peak of competitive trail running. First held in 2003, with a 171-km (106-mile) course with 10,000m (33,000ft) of elevation, it is as gruelling in the effort demanded as it is gorgeous in the views delivered. It's an iconic race because of the beauty that you experience, both in terms of the scenery and the difficulty of the course. With a limit of 2,300 runners, it's literally not for everyone, but once you climb those mountains, the view is picture perfect. It's the polar opposite of running through smoggy city streets.

Beyond the original tour around the Mont Blanc massif, there is a UTMB World Series that has over 50 races around the world. Seen as emblematic of the exponential growth and commercialization of trail, many prominent figures in the trail running world have been outspoken about the business tactics of UTMB and their partners.

OPPOSITE

The start line at the UTMB.

Office de Tourisme
FINISHER
SUUNTO
CHAMONIX-MONT-BLANC
HOKA
FLY HUMAN FLY
HOKA UTMB MONT-BLANC
HOKA UTMB MONT-BLANC
HOKA
FLY HUMAN FLY
SUUNTO
HOKA
FLY HUMAN FLY
HOKA UTMB MONT-BLANC

The Barkley Marathons

On 23 March 2024 running was making headlines on the BBC News website. I'm not talking about the sport section – it was the top story across all news, ahead of even the Princess of Wales's cancer diagnosis. Jasmin Paris became the first woman to complete the Barkley Marathons, a feat that only 19 people had previously managed since 1986.

If races like Boston, Western States and The Speed Project add obstacles to their entry process, getting into the Barkley Marathons is a completely opaque process. That's partly because park officials only allow 35 runners to run through Frozen Head State Park every year, but also because founder Gary 'Lazarus Lake' Cantrell is a true outsider. Indeed, the race is started when Cantrell lights a ceremonial cigarette, and he changes the course difficulty every year depending on previous year's results.

One of the reasons it was so impressive that Jasmin Paris finished the course is that Cantrell once suggested that no woman could ever win his race. Importantly, men also don't meet his standards. With five loops of the unmarked, unsupported course required to complete the 100-mile race within 60 hours, it is incredibly difficult. Anyone completing three loops gets a figurative pat on the head by calling that achievement a Fun Run. Cantrell created the race after learning that James Earl Ray, Martin Luther King Jr's murderer, spent 54 hours in the state park after escaping from Brushy Mountain State Penitentiary but only covered 8 miles (13km). From questionable beginnings has come greatness.

OPPOSITE

'Lazarus Lake' at the famous gate at the Barkley Marathons.

OVERLEAF

Jasmin Paris collapses triumphantly after completing the 2024 Barkley Marathons.

DO NOT
BLOCK GATE

HAUL

Western States Endurance Run

The world's oldest 100-mile (161-km) race is the Boston Marathon of American trail running, with a 1 per cent chance of getting into the race via the ballot. If you enter every year, expect to wait seven years to finally be able to traverse California's Sierra Nevada Mountains with 374 others.

The first event was held in 1977 with 16 runners, but only one runner completed the 100 miles within 24 hours. Taking place in the last weekend of June each year, it's the most competitive ultramarathon in the USA due to the rugged terrain, which includes 18,000ft (5,500m) of vertical elevation, a river crossing and wildly disparate temperatures, which range from icy mountain cold to sweltering desert heat.

Hal Koerner, the winner of the WS100 in both 2007 and 2009, considers the race to be truly unique: 'There is no comparison between Wimbledon and Key Biscayne, the Masters and the Tucson Open or the Olympic 1500m and the Bowerman Mile. The pressure to perform at Western States is unlike any other ultra in the world, and the effects of pressure on performance in my mind is greater than any other single factor. More than the climbing and descents, or the scorching heat of the canyons. It doesn't matter if you're vying for first place or finishing your first 100, Western States holds its runners in the highest esteem; just be ready to do the same for the race.'

OPPOSITE

Dan Barger crests 8,300ft during the 36th annual Western States Endurance Run.

Team
SUBARU
98

Parkrun

One of the most significant running movements in the world started with 13 friends having the idea to run 5km around Bushy Park in south-west London back in 2004. The genesis of parkrun came from founder Paul Sinton-Hewitt's desire to spend more time with his running friends; these days, considerably more than 13 people run 5km every Saturday morning.

Now there are over 2,000 parkrun events in 23 countries around the world, with over 800 locations all over the UK, where over a quarter of a million people log a parkrun time every Saturday morning. The community aspect is furthered by the fact that almost 50,000 volunteers (every week!) make parkrun events go smoothly. With over 10 million registered runners, it's a true phenomenon that led to significant growth in running in the UK, boosted by Boris Johnson, when he was Mayor of London, forming an initiative to have a parkrun in every one of London's 32 boroughs. He believed in the wide-ranging benefits of exercise for everyone, and the accessibility of both jogging and parkrun made it an obvious choice.

OPPOSITE

Parkrunners in Bushy Park, London.

Sri Chinmoy Marathon Self-Transcendence 3,100-Mile Race

One of the more curious races to occur each year takes place around the same New York City block every single summer, and at 3,100 miles (around 5,000km), it's the longest certified footrace in the world. Yes, 5,649 times around a single block. You have 52 days to perform the feat, averaging at least 59.62 miles (95.95km) every day, but you might look at a track or treadmill differently afterwards.

Running your first marathon is a life-defining event, and running 100m as fast as you can is a beautifully succinct gauge of speed, but running around a nondescript, grey city block in Queens for over seven weeks? Why would you want to do that? Well, you have to explain that in the application, and the organizers look for applicants who fulfil the character traits of wanting to test their mental and spiritual aptitude, once their 'physical prowess has reached its limit'.

OPPOSITE

Andrea Marcato of Italy after winning the race in 2021.

3100
ANDREA
Self-Transcendence

HEALTH IS WEALTH

They say that money can't buy happiness, but research shows that in the USA 73 per cent of runners earn 50 per cent over the median salary. That suggests that health and wealth may be linked, but it also begs the follow-up question: how closely related are health and happiness?

We've all heard about the virtues and benefits of maintaining good health from a young age. We should try to eat healthy food more often than not to maintain a balanced diet, and try to get enough high-quality sleep every night. We should drink water, reduce stress and brush our teeth. And we should stay active. We're taught these ideas at school, during physical education classes, as well as being one of the basics of as many sports as possible, including athletics or cross-country. The hope is that one of them will light a fire in a young heart, and that person will go on to maintain that discipline for life.

The American Heart Association has long been prescribing at least 150 minutes of moderate activity per week, with 300 minutes recommended for increased benefits. The UK's National Health Service mirrors this messaging. The goal is to maintain good cardiovascular health in a society where sedentary jobs have increased by 83 per cent since 1950.

It's been an issue for a while. For a full four weeks of 1985, Britain indulged in the most elaborate public health campaign in its history. Centred around the Great British Fun Run, a massive 2,200-mile (3,540-km) relay that travelled the length and breadth of England, Wales, and Scotland, visiting 87 health festivals en route. A million people took part in the festivities, and jogging was at the heart of the whole endeavour.

OPPOSITE

Sebastian Coe carries the 'health charter' as he begins the world's longest relay race.

TV
versus
leukaemia
GREAT FUN
BRITISH RUN
D2
D3

RUNNING I
A NATURAI
NON-DIGIT
OF BUILDI

S

,

ÅL WAY

IG BONDS

In that context, it's no surprise that we've been living in an undulating, but ever-rising, running boom for the past three decades. Every level of race from America's favourite 5K, the Thanksgiving morning Turkey Trot, to the major marathons around the world have been selling out with increasing frequency.

Part of the current popularity of running is Couch to 5K. The concept was quietly published by American web developer Josh Clark on his personal website in 1996, with a goal of providing a freely accessible training plan to get would-be runners off the couch and running for 30 minutes straight, or completing a 5km run in just nine weeks. After starting to run during a period of personal strife, he was encouraged by the discomfort and slowness dissipating over time, and wanted to share a gentler version of his experience with others. It's no coincidence that a concept born of pure intention became one of the world's most popular exercise programmes. After being used successfully by over 5 million people in its first 20 years, the NHS took the idea and partnered with the BBC in 2016 to design a groundbreaking free fitness app, which has been downloaded 7 million times since launch, with a record 8.7 million Couch to 5K runs completed in 2024 alone.

The beauty of that training plan is its simplicity, and who doesn't crave the easiest path to health? In this brave new world of injectable anti-aging serums, and testing-based biohacking with a view to achieve immortality, it's going for a jog that the research shows can give you extra years of life – maybe up to a decade. Multiple studies have shown that running regularly, for 30 to 40 minutes, four or five times a week, can positively affect the parts of our DNA that mark our biological age. These telomeres shorten as we get older, and running slows that process down. You may well joke that you spend those extra years running, so why bother, but the increase in quality of life is worth it, isn't it? Feeling better, happier, more accomplished, healthier.

The mental health benefits are an increasingly large part of the conversation. We've always known about taking a walk to clear your head, and exercise has long been recommended as a treatment for depression, but any formal education around mental wellness is a truly modern phenomenon.

OVERLEAF

Judge Craig Mitchell leading the Skid Row
Running Club in Los Angeles.

The Individuals with Disabilities Education Act has been around in the USA in some form since the 1970s, but it wasn't until 1997 that it was expanded to supporting students with emotional and behavioural disabilities. This led to more mental health professionals becoming involved at the school level, with New York passing legislation to require mental health education in schools in 2016. Talking about mental health became less taboo, and a whole generation of children has grown up not only with less stigma around discussing their psychological well-being, but also a greater understanding of what they need, and when they need it.

In an era where, in 2023, the American Surgeon General declared a loneliness epidemic across the country, social running can be a solution. In 2024, 21 per cent of Americans reported serious feelings of loneliness, while 7 per cent of those in the UK had those feelings in 2022 – up a percentage point from 2020. Loneliness has been strongly linked to having a negative impact on your mental health, contributing to increased depression and anxiety, and two things were put into perspective by the Covid pandemic: the importance of being able to socialize; and the importance of comfortable solitude.

On the one hand, it's no surprise that social run clubs have proliferated with such speed in recent years. It's so easy to have a chat when you're running side by side, without eye contact, euphoric hormones coursing through your body like nature's social serum. With no other distractions in that moment, you are forced to be completely present. In a completely connected world, running is a natural, non-digital way of building bonds. Running on your own can offer completely different but similarly dramatic and complementary benefits.

Once you cut through the sounds of your environment, the silence can be uncomfortable. You have to be alone with your thoughts, and you have to learn to become comfortable with them, but solitude is a place where you can disconnect and increase self-awareness. You can use this alone time to quietly improve your emotional regulation, and you will gain confidence from it. When you have nobody else to rely on, your decision-making instincts simply *have* to improve. Solo running and the associated solitude is a worthy practice that can aid self-discovery and help combat loneliness.

'All I do is keep on running in my own cozy, homemade void, my own nostalgic silence. And this is a pretty wonderful thing. No matter what anybody else says,' says Haruki Murakami, who writes frequently about spending time with only himself in *What I Talk About When I Talk About Running*.

THE PURSUIT OF HAPPINESS

Something that few will argue about wanting and needing is happiness. Both Hungarian-American psychologist Mihaly Csikszentmihalyi and Swiss psychoanalyst Carl Jung spent their academic lives searching for the key to happiness. While their approaches differed, their work overlapped greatly.

Jung believed that a fulfilling life came from self-discovery, to become as true a version of oneself as possible, while in the 1990s, Csikszentmihalyi identified the flow state – a period of deep focus while engaging in an activity, like running – as the method to achieve the most productive, creative and happy version of oneself. It's the moment of clarity while you're running where your limbs almost feel automated, where the friction required to force movement in your body is minimal. Your travel to your destination is understood, allowing you to be fully present in the moment. Happy.

In one very specific group of people's quest for happiness, running provides a level of support they can't find in wider society. Judge Craig Mitchell, a Superior Court Judge in Los Angeles who founded Skid Row Running Club in 2012 to use 'the power of running to improve the lives of those who are at risk of homelessness and addiction', talks about running being 'a healthier addiction' to what many in his marathon training programme have previously suffered. He talks about committing to a dedicated running programme being just one part of the recovery programme support system, alongside group therapy sessions, individual counselling and 12-step meetings. Mitchell believes that all of this is required to help people fully reintegrate into society. That support not being provided by the state is why he created Skid Row Running Club – to involve the wider community in helping an area of severe homelessness in Los Angeles that is just half a square mile (about a square kilometre) in size, but has a population density greater than that of New York.

If running at its worst is better than anyone's rock bottom, it's still important to understand what the few relative negatives can be. It could be as simple as wondering how hot is too hot or at what point on the air-quality index running a marathon switches from an extremely strenuous endeavour to being a life-threatening event – but there's more to it. While moderate activity has been shown to boost immunity, extreme efforts, such as running a marathon, can actually blunt the immune system for a few days afterwards, leaving the runner more susceptible to infection and viruses in the days following the race, and ultramarathoners have been shown to have post-race levels of inflammation in the blood similar to people with cancer or cirrhosis. Those inflammation levels also returned to normal within a week, showing how remarkable the body is at recovering after massive exertion.

Something else that running a marathon famously does to your body is burn fat reserves, but maybe not from where you might suspect. Studies show that during extra-long-distance efforts, the fats burned are in your brain. These fats, called myelin, are important for electrical conduction in the brain, and their removal can result in symptoms like loss of motor coordination, sensory integration and emotional processing, which can go some way to explaining why people running ultramarathons in particular can begin to suffer hallucinations and the loss of certain senses.

Just as the inflammation levels and immune system recover, these myelin fats return to normal levels within a couple of months, which could be important to consider in a training plan or personal race calendar. Good training includes building an awareness of your body's limits, and the improved data and research that we have available to us now has allowed for much better tailored plans.

We've reached a point in society, science and culture where health doesn't only mean cardiovascular fitness and having a BMI within a certain range. The separation of mental and physical health has never made sense. We've long understood the connections of body and mind or soul, with ancient practices like yoga, which is a wonderful complement to running, involving every part of a person. While the old proverb of 'health is wealth' was adopted by run clubs many years ago, we're now in a glorious age where we can understand and embrace both the physical and mental benefits of running, and if you can figure out how to run your way towards happiness, you'll be living a rich life.

Josh Clark

Creator of Couch to 5K

The nine-week-long beginner's running programme was created in 1996 by Josh Clark, an American web developer and designer, and has helped millions begin and connect on their running journeys. Now C25K is an official exercise app provided to the British public for free by the NHS in conjunction with the BBC.

WHY DID YOU CREATE THE COUCH TO 5K SCHEDULE?
I had done that journey from couch to 5K and I didn't enjoy how I got there, but when I got to the other side of it, I was like, 'This feels good'. There has to be a gentler way for people to discover the joy and pleasure and happiness of running, because too many people just associate it with pain and boredom. I felt like there's got to be a better way to go from a non-runner to a runner.

WHAT HAS BEEN THE GREATEST LEGACY OF THE PROGRAMME?
It feels hands down – aside from being a parent – the most meaningful thing that I'll likely do in my life. Through a series of accidents it became this commonly understood and shared key to getting started that's been shared by millions of people. It's something that I am really proud of, even though I also recognize that the accomplishment of it actually belongs to all the people who have followed the schedule.

What's exciting about it to me personally is that here's a system or platform that can enable others to do or become something more than they may have expected of themselves. I get a lot of email messages from people who have completed C25K and the notes are rarely about finishing their first 5K. It's often things like, 'I did this thing that I didn't think was possible for me, and it's changed the way that I think about myself.' That touches the heart.

WHAT ONLINE FEATURES HELPED C25K THRIVE?

I think one of the early vectors for Couch to 5K is that the site that I built had a little discussion forum that grew and grew. People started sharing and following the schedule together online. While I created the schedule in 1996, it really took off with the rise of Facebook, as a very portable schedule where people could talk about being on week 3 day 2, and there was a kind of shorthand that emerged for sharing and supporting each other.

WHY DO YOU THINK C25K BECAME SO POPULAR?

For a lot of people who are in that position, and see themselves there, which is where I was, they often have a history of defeat with fitness, and that comes at an early age. A bad physical fitness programme at school. This idea that many of us grow up with, that, 'I'm not an athlete. That's not for me. My body can't do this.'

I think real braveness is overcoming that really strong association of, 'I am not a runner,' that's often coming from some kind of crisis or unhappiness with yourself or your life that makes you start doing this. People generally don't go into C25K excited about running or feeling good about themselves, and the remarkable thing that happens over the course of these nine weeks is that it changes their perception of not only the sport, but of themselves, which is a powerful thing.

Allie Bailey

Author and UK Coach of the Year 2024

British ultrarunner and coach Allie Bailey battled back from addiction to write one of the most disarming running books of recent years, *There is No Wall*, and specializes in training the minds of the 'ultra lost and ultra curious'.

WHY DID YOU START RUNNING?

Working in music, alcohol was everywhere all of the time. I was very depressed, so I thought, 'I'm gonna start running because running's really good for your mental health,' so I did. I'm expecting something to happen like, 'Oh, I run now, so maybe I'll get better; magically just not feel awful,' but that didn't happen.

HOW HAS THERAPY HELPED YOU AS A RUNNER?

A lot of the stuff you're taught in therapy when you're not well, you can use on a hill, and if you can use it on a hill, you can use it at home. The running will give you the tools and the environment to test strategies, to test your resilience, and to test fear. If you start running and you think, 'If I feel this bad now, how am I going to feel in x miles? How am I going to get to the end?' come right back to the moment. You don't know how you're gonna feel in 5 miles. All you can do is control what's going on in the moment. If you feel tired, slow down. If you feel hungry, have something to eat. If you feel bored, put your headphones on. Just be in that moment and don't think 15 steps ahead.

ARE THERE ANY MENTAL HEALTH DOWNSIDES TO RUNNING?

The amount of clients I have who can't hit a certain time and they're like, 'It's making me so depressed and really anxious.' I tell them they're running for

leisure time, and should be enjoying it. It takes a really long time to unpick that, but it's all based in the idea of success.

When you're worrying that you're not fast enough, or that Dave from accounts is quicker than you, that's not going to help your anxiety. I want to illustrate to people that if you use running for the right reason - as a place to test the stuff, and as a place to keep your brain and your mind healthy - it's great. If you're using it to prove something, there's every likelihood that it's not going to work out that well for you.

THE TECH REVOLUTION

At its most essential, running will always just be the runner and the run they're on that day, but we're a species of addicts, and our newest addiction is to technology. According to multiple studies between 2020 and 2025, half of Americans are addicted to their phones, with between 5 and 10 per cent severely addicted to the internet. It makes sense that the act of running - the most human of activities - is also littered with gadgets and trinkets.

The speed at which tech is now integrated with the world means that we have to stay nimble and curious in order to change effectively with it. It would be cute to think back on previous eras with rose-tinted glasses, saying that we just didn't care about the numbers before this, that we just pulled on a pair of shorts and ran for health or tradition in the olden days, but it wouldn't be true. Even in the 1980s, there was enough demand for logging accurate times to implement radio chips into race bibs. Before that, 20th-century technological innovation included rubber soles on shoes, and the introduction of frame-by-frame camera technology on finish lines. We have *always* looked to innovate the sport with the latest technological advancements. Yes, there is hyper-accurate GPS now, and automated training regimens, but there is also mass communication, and listening to music on the go is second nature.

Listening to music while running is a hugely popular thing to do, of course, with a 2016 *Runner's World* survey finding that 75 per cent of the 3,523 runners they spoke to were in favour of listening to music. Improvements in technology over time have only made that more possible. Time and again studies have shown that listening to music can improve running performance by boosting mood and providing motivation. Due to the relaxing effect of jamming a well-curated playlist, listening to music could even lower your blood lactate levels, resulting in an increase in your speed and distance. Songs played

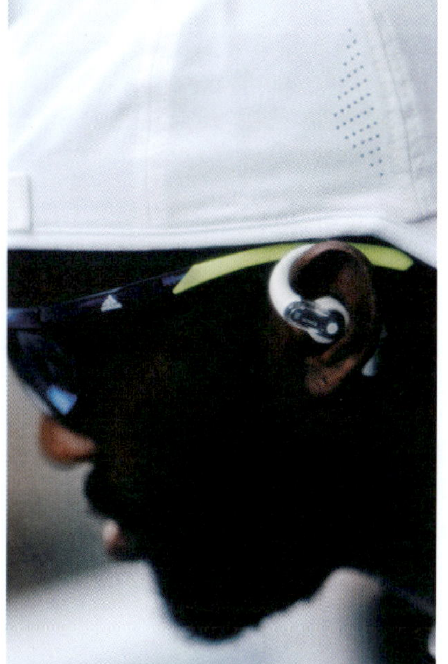

ABOVE

Earbuds for listening to music on the go.

at 130 beats per minute can help you maintain a metronomic cadence, and the style of music you choose can help you either speed up or slow down, depending on what kind of run you're planning on doing. Dance music or heavy metal can energize your pace, while classical music can calm you for a long, easy effort.

Whatever your evidence-based reasoning, prior to 2000 you had to be really desperate to listen to music while running because you'd have to clip a cumbersome Walkman or portable CD player to your waistband. The physical relic known as a compact disc was jolted with every step, making the listening experience a stuttering mess. The move to digital music first allowed us to clip a smaller MP3 player somewhere onto our person, but the big upgrade was having skip-free music, and even that improved when we could just use our phones or load the music onto our smartwatches. Ditching the wires was also a big move brought about by the variety of wireless earbuds, with a special mention to bone-conducting headphones that allow you to listen to music or podcasts while also maintaining awareness of your surroundings, which is as useful for dodging cars while running through an inner city as it is for listening out for cows or bears out in the countryside. Both types of threat are equally unpredictable.

That all started to happen at the end of the 20th century, when the Third Industrial Revolution AKA the digital revolution descended upon us, signalling the onset of constant technological advances that drastically changed our daily lives. We got personal computers, and then we got the internet, and then smartphones improved so much that we now have our own internet-ready computers on our person at all times. And to think that we crept into the year 2000 on tiptoes, fearing that all of our new-fangled electronic devices would combust in a fury of digital screeching. Could the machines' internal timepieces handle this brave new world with dates that started 20–? It quickly turned out, of course, that they could.

Cut to the present day and, while every running watch has its own native app, it's Strava, founded in 2009 as a cycling-oriented social network, that runners meticulously log their activities on, displaying their distances, average paces, elapsed times and heart-rate zones for all to see.

SO MUCH DATA

The result of giving increasing amounts of biometric data to a society that's encouraged to optimize every single moment of their lives fits neatly into the idea of the 'quantified self'. That's the cultural phenomenon of self-tracking with technology that was first noticed in the 1970s, but was formalized by the editors of technology magazine *Wired*, Gary Wolf and Kevin Kelly, in 2007 when it became clear quite how much data humans were generating about themselves. As we are able to measure every part of our lives, we are able to focus more and more on the minutiae of our lives, whether it's a goal of walking 10,000 steps a day, logged effortlessly by our watches or phones, or running 80 per cent of our 50 weekly miles with our heart rates at a consistently low intensity – where you can have a conversation, for instance. The technology, and the daily public conversations that that new tech has allowed us to have, has ushered in a new age of personal science as we constantly bio-hack our marginal gains.

Whether you're wearing a separate heart-rate monitor, or you're logging your run using your phone, Strava will ping your data to the feeds of everyone you're connected to. There were some questions about who *should* see your data when activity heatmaps around previously unmapped military bases were published in 2018, highlighting the all too new concern of digital privacy. Remember: having this amount of information at our fingertips is brand new to *this* generation. There is no guidebook for how to share your data publicly. Consider the possible repercussions of someone absent-mindedly sharing the route that they run every day at seven o'clock in the morning. Consider that they're first broadcasting that their home may be empty at that time every day, but also exactly where they will be. Danger could await in both situations.

On the other end of the spectrum of being worried, it might be nice to know that the depth of big data that Strava collects from its users is being used for good. With all the kudos, corporate challenges, club runs and carefully angled mid-run photos, Strava can seem like just another social network, but there is a department called Strava Metro that has been using our timed GPS-mapped activities to provide anonymized data sets to the non-profit community. For over a decade, city planners, departments of transport and academic researchers around the world have been using this information with the heady goal of improving local infrastructure to make cities more accessible, more efficient and safer for all.

EVERY RU
STRAVA IS
LITTLE ST
THAT RUN

N ON
A TINY
ORY ABOUT
NER

It was a brilliantly effective way for run clubs to connect to members, and vice versa. They grew organically, and fast. It was another highly engaging way that leveraged the power of online community to help runners choose Strava over the native app for their running watches, and so Strava duly became the number-one hotspot for runners to post their runs and compare their stats.

Every run on Strava is a tiny little story about that runner, and the digital revolution's software explosion has hugely impacted storytelling, especially as the Influencer Era started to bloom in 2010. We've always had influencers, of course, but the big players in the internet's cult of personalities used to be bloggers and MySpace luminaries. As YouTube (2005) and Instagram (2010) hit the app stores, the ease with which runners' stories could be told via those tiny screens in all of our pockets democratized this part of the world, and when TikTok came to America in 2017, a whole new wave of influencers specializing in engaging their audiences with short-form niche video content was born.

It's true in running, as it is in life, that technology has fundamentally impacted our lives on all levels, altering every facet of our daily motions. It's allowed us to do more of everything. Our communications are faster on both a personal and public level, and – for better or for worse – the way we are able to receive information has changed completely. Is it too much? That's for an individual to work out, but just as some are trading in their smartphones for retro flip phones in an attempt to get back to basics, some runners are ditching their smartwatches for a timepiece that does nothing more than tell the time.

The fact is that we're living through a revolution and, for all the benefits, a lot of the behaviour that has become normalized since carrying smartphones around in our pockets all the time is sometimes neither the healthiest nor the safest. The technology, though, is going nowhere, so it's up to us to engage with it in the best possible way.

OPPOSITE

A 1998 advert for a Panasonic portable CD player.

Sound's personal.
Jog it
SHOCK WAVE
Jolt it. Pound it.
Panasonic introduces the first portable CD jogger system.*
Strap it on, pull the sport belt tight and take off. It virtually eliminates the skips and delivers continuous tunes. It's the first system that lets you listen to your CDs while you jog, so demand it. (It's not that we're telling you what to listen to, we're telling you how to listen to it better.)
www.panasonic.com/audio
Panasonic
Panasonic
Panasonic
just slightly ahead of our time
*System consists of:
Shockwave portable CD player and neoprene sport belt • Anti-Shock Memory II – our best anti-skip system ever • Energy saving system extends battery life •
For more info call 800/211-PANA

THE GENESIS OF THE LOCAL LEGEND

There was one event in 2010, however, that served as a watershed moment for how we would use mobile tech within our running practices to satisfy our hunger for self-monitoring and improvement, and that was Grid. It hasn't gone down in folklore as an iconic event by any means, but the influence of the two-week-long challenge is clear because the knock-on effects and features it included are now second nature to us. The fusion of virtual, real-time documentation of scintillating competition made a new horizon seem possible. Running became about the game.

It started with a problem that had been identified by Nike: while there were plenty of young people running in cities, they weren't yet thinking of themselves as runners. It was a cultural disconnect that the largest sportswear brand in the world was determined to remedy, and their solution was to turn London into a board game. You had to run it to win it. It was geocaching but for running, and they called it Grid. 'Claim your streets', came the challenge.

Notably, the concept came from the team at Wieden+Kennedy, Nike's creative agency of choice. They are still one of the largest independent advertising agencies in the world, and were early supporters of New York's Bridgerunners, the chaotic Lower Manhattan run crew that sparked a bold new generation of unorthodox urban runners. Graeme Douglas was working at Wieden+Kennedy when he came up with the idea of Grid, and talks of a time before we had gaming at our fingertips, and precise location data.

'We wanted to give people ownership and just wanted to make running feel more fun,' Douglas explains. 'If we talked to people that were obsessed with gaming metrics about competition and running, they'd think about racing and marathons. They definitely wouldn't think about running between two phone boxes in a postcode to win a game.'

The city was broken up into 48 postal codes, and each zone had four British Telecom phone boxes that were distinctively rebranded by Nike. The mission was to run between phone boxes – some were over 6 miles (10km) apart, some

OPPOSITE

A runner starts their watch.

were 200 yards (180m) – with players logging their entries at each point by calling a number and entering their identifying number via the keypad. Rankings could be found on the official website, and any badges accrued would appear on your Facebook profile. The winners would be celebrated on billboards in the neighbourhoods they'd conquered. There was pride to be displayed both publicly and within your friend group. It was all about kudos.

'The way apps now work instantly, none of that existed back then,' Douglas reminisces excitedly. 'A lot of people got involved with Grid. If you look at the running apps now, they've all got gamification built into their fundamentals.'

We're up to 90 per cent-plus ownership now in the USA and UK, but in 2010 smartphone usage was still growing, with almost a third of US adults owning one. The major social media website visited back then was Facebook, but GPS accuracy was an issue. While open areas could yield accuracy of less than 10 yards/metres, if there was any height, like dense forestry, or in urban areas such as London, accuracy could be ten times worse. Pre-digital infrastructure was the solution: phone boxes. In direct correlation with the uptake of smartphones, phone boxes were being used less and less, with usage in the UK halving between 2005 and 2008, according to Ofcom data.

All of these ideas and observations came together to devise Grid. The still-iconic phone boxes removed the technological barriers to playing the game, improved location data, and made the game a quintessentially London event. It was a mish-mash hybrid amalgamation of GPS gamification of real-life running and online bragging, with the potential to get your face on a billboard. By requiring time, desire and technical nous, Grid was the perfect way to make running a buzzy activity with the younger generation.

After testing the idea in a one-day event around the 2010 London Marathon, Nike launched a 15-day challenge in October of that year that almost 3,000 runners participated in, completing over 30,000 runs and 12,500 miles (20,000km). Some players even tried to run in all 48 postcodes. While it was a hugely successful event, there were no further editions due to the rapid improvement of smartphone technology at the time, but the stories that were told and the kudos that was dished out to those local legends will last forever.

The success of the project led directly to a new digital services division at Nike HQ, and the development of one of the first runner-specific pieces of wearable technology. There were other pioneers in the sector such as Jawbone and FitBit, but the partnerships that an established incumbent such as Nike could hold should've put the American sportswear giant ahead of any upstarts. They had already been working closely with fellow West Coasters, Apple, on integrating music with their running app and with TomTom on a general GPS exercise watch, but the Nike+ Fuelband connected wirelessly to the Nike+ app. It should've been a game-changer, but it ultimately failed due to a variety of reasons and was discontinued. Regardless, Grid's legacy still paved the way to forever change the way we devour and publicly display our running metrics.

OPPOSITE

Photo finish technology shows Usain Bolt winning the 100m final at the 2008 Olympic Games.

Laura Green

Influencer and comedian

Known as Laura McGreen on Instagram, the Boston-based social media influencer brings humour to topics like women's sports, parenthood and being a 'washed-up collegiate athlete'.

WHAT HAS INSTAGRAM ALLOWED YOU TO DO?

I rose quickly enough to quit my physical therapy job within three months of starting. I was expecting to get a paycheck, and the ability to travel to cool races around the world, but I didn't think about this sweet, genuine community of runners that have rallied around me. When I had my third baby, I went on Instagram, and I said, 'Listen, I can't really take time off because you have to feed the algorithm to maintain relevance, so I'm going to post old videos. If you have the time to engage with these videos, that helps me a ton.' Those videos have done better than any other videos I've ever posted, and all I had to do was ask for help.

HOW IMPORTANT IS IT TO TELL THE KINDS OF STORIES YOU TELL?

People ask me if my parents ran. They didn't. I don't know that my mom knew that running was a thing that she *could* do. That has changed over the years. I can show my own kids how women and sports go hand in hand, and if you keep showcasing women who are doing really cool things, whether it be at the elite level or they're starting a run crew or they're working towards some incredible cause, and they're using running as their vehicle, even if it's just me making silly videos over and over again, it's an act of resistance. It's showing people that our bodies deserve to be out there and deserve to be safe.

WHAT ARE THE NEGATIVES OF TELLING STORIES ABOUT WOMEN ONLINE?

I got into a bad comment section online the other day – I shouldn't have – and I ended up scrolling, and reading these terrible comments about how everyone watches women's sports, and men are like, 'Actually, they don't'. This is the fight. Hockey is not my number-one sport to watch, so I just don't watch it. Do I go online and talk about how it's not a real sport? Do I go on to try and trash it, and talk about soccer is a 'real sport', and bring the players down? No. I just don't watch it, and that's OK. We are still just constantly batting away the haters, and it's like ... just ignore us!

THE RISE OF THE SUPER SHOE

It was the final day of the 2016 Olympic Games in Rio de Janeiro, Brazil, when the biggest technological change in running made a subtle debut. Nike quietly but emphatically unveiled the shoe that would change the face of distance running forever when all three medallists standing on the podium of the men's marathon event were wearing a Vaporfly prototype.

It was a few short months later that Nike formally announced the Vaporfly 4% – the first ever super shoe. Aimed at elite and very, very serious road runners, it hit the headlines due to the claim of improving one's running economy by 4 per cent. The theory states that if you require less energy to achieve a certain pace, you will be able to go faster for longer, and break more records – personal or official. That immediately captured the attention of every single prospective Boston-qualifier wannabe amateur runner out there. When seconds matter in terms of reaching the threshold time, 4 per cent given to you for free was enormous. Sure, the shoes cost $250, and they were rumoured to last just a fraction of the miles of regular shoes, but you were already buying the best shoes anyway. What price could you really place on a 4 per cent improvement?

Nike's immediate goal was to demonstrate how good the shoes really were by helping the 2016 Olympic marathon winner Eliud Kipchoge use that 4 per cent mechanical boost to finally breach the sub-two-hour marathon in Project Breaking2. The marathon world record at the time was 2:02:57, registered by Dennis Kimetto in Berlin in 2014. Nike's plan was to create a race with optimal conditions. Everything from the climate and the altitude to in-race provisions such as a pacing cart with the time displayed and multiple top-level athletes taking turns in pacing, providing both fresh legs and a human

OPPOSITE

Kipchoge in Project Breaking2.

windbreaker for Kipchoge. They held the event on the race track in Monza, Italy, in May 2017, but it was ultimately unsuccessful. Despite all the help and planning, Kipchoge clocked 2:00:25 on the day. Regardless that these non-standard conditions made any result ineligible for a true world record, the fact that Nike and Kipchoge tried to find the next human limit inspired those watching intently to try that little bit harder. They gave runners hope.

The Kenyan did eventually get that elusive 1:59:40 time at another meticulously planned event in Vienna in October 2019, but even if he hadn't, the sub-two-hour marathon would still have forever been intrinsically linked to him (and the Vaporfly) in the same way the 4-minute mile belongs to Roger Bannister. Immortality achieved, albeit with the caveat of coming via nouveau carbon-plated midsole technology.

There was some initial conversation - if not outrage - during this time as questions were asked about the role of technology in sports, claiming 'mechanical doping' in this instance, but we've now firmly settled into this bold new era of running shoes. It took until 2020 for World Athletics to implement an actual rule restricting the maximum sole thickness in races to 40mm (just over an inch and a half), but since the majority of fastest marathon times since 2017 have been set while wearing super shoes, we're living in a new era where the world record requires a delineator of before or after the super shoe.

By the time the Vaporfly was released, Hoka was already making waves with their maximal cushioning in trail shoes designed for softening the effects of downhills on runners' lower limbs, but Nike really took it to the next level by introducing the springy, novel carbon plate to a new, extremely lightweight foam. Prior to the Vaporfly, fast marathons were run while wearing the lightest shoes possible, which involved as little cushioning as possible. The 2015 Boston Marathon was won by Lelisa Desisa, who wore the firm-soled Nike Zoom Streak 3. No foam wedges under the heels of those racing flats, which focused instead on a grippier outsole.

OPPOSITE

Lelisa Desisa after winning the Boston Marathon in 2015.

THE BOSTON MARATHON

RACING FL
PRIOR TO
WERE A P
BEAST

ATS
972
IMITIVE

Racing flats prior to 1972 were a primitive beast, with as little going into them as possible. Bill Bowerman and Nike looked to solve the stress fractures and other injuries those shoes were being blamed for with new plush cushioning, that was then blamed for ... giving runners stress fractures and other injuries. And so the barefoot era duly entered the picture in the 2000s, and Chris McDougall's *Born to Run* bestseller spawned a minimalist shoe craze. It's a clear cycle, which suggests we might expect to see less cushioning again in the future, but it's severely unlikely that the recreational runner will ever want to give up the comfort of plush cushioning or the energy rebound of carbon plates. We're doing this for fun, after all.

IT'S ONE PAIR OF SHOES – WHAT COULD IT COST?

With carbon-plated marathon shoes sitting at almost $300 (£240), the 4 per cent of extra performance the new shoes on the block promise cost 50 per cent more. It's a steep price, but with the $16.50 minimum wage in California, you can buy a pair with a couple of days of hard work, and maybe get an ice cream on the way home. But what if those same shoes cost you $7,500? You might think twice about pushing your marathon efforts.

Transport your mind, for a moment, to a country where the average monthly income is $220, which is just over 4 per cent of the average Californian monthly income of $5,200. When confronted with the option of spending six weeks of salary to buy a brand-new pair of premium running shoes, you start to understand what a luxury item they really are to some. That's the case in Bangladesh, where my parents emigrated from to the UK. The shoes cost the same, but the relative spending power is not. That so many people are employed in manufacturing sportswear in countries like Bangladesh and Vietnam is not lost on me.

It wouldn't be possible for Nike to sell shoes in Bangladesh at a price proportional to the salary there (say $12?), or else people in countries with higher salaries would simply buy their running shoes from there, and Nike would cease to be a company worth $30 billion. The end result is that people in countries like Bangladesh are stuck choosing between exorbitant prices and rock-bottom options. You can still run in a no-name brand, of course, but the technology and engineering – and hence performance benefits – contained in your Pegasuses and Ultraboosts are very, very real.

Sajjad Hossain Snigdho, a 2:42 marathoner and certified coach from Bangladesh's capital city, Dhaka, talks about the vicious circle that means that buying power will remain limited, even for more promising athletes than him. While Bangladesh has competed in every summer Olympics since 1984, they have not won a single medal, so it's impossible for home-grown coaches to claim that pedigree. Without top coaches, the top athletes lack the guidance and infrastructure to become sporting superstars, even at the national level, where they compete for sponsorship money with athletes from the popular sports of cricket and soccer.

Contrary to all the narratives about running being a low-cost hobby, and accepting that shoes *are* still the only piece of necessary equipment, in Bangladesh running is an extremely expensive hobby. When the science says that the midsole cushioning on a pair of modern running shoes starts to degrade after 350 miles (500km), the costs for endurance runners goes up even more. Logging 50 miles (80km) or more per week during marathon training will wear a pair out in under two months, so going through six pairs of running shoes a year is very possible as a distance runner. Apportioning up to half of one's annual salary on just the shoes is less unconscionable and more bordering on the absurd. Runners are prone to absurdity, but that is taking it to the next level. What's the solution, then?

Snigdho tells me how he makes a pair of shoes last four times as long as recommended, registering 1,250 miles (2,000km) in them. As the shoe loses its cushioning, you invite injury as the impact felt through your joints increases. The flattened shoes mean your foot strikes the ground differently, changing your gait, thus stressing your body differently, inviting injury another way. Therein lies another problem: if the money is paid for the benefits of the midsole cushioning, but you're only reaping those benefits for a quarter of the time that you're wearing them, is it really worth buying the better shoes at all?

Perhaps. But there is another factor to consider. With the amount of time runners spend outdoors, it makes sense that we would like to care for it, but our steady, inevitable consumption of running shoes is the single worst thing that runners can do for the environment. However, there is a move towards sustainable practices in the running shoe world. Dutch company 4T2 has made replacing both the outsole and insole possible from their Amsterdam atelier,

and champion mountain runner Kilian Jornet's Nnormal shoes are designed around the idea of high-quality modular, replaceable components. More recently, On's innovative LightSpray technology, which 'forms a complete $330 shoe upper in a single, three-minute step', is said to reduce carbon emissions by 75 per cent. Like $80,000 electric cars, custom shoes might be the key to a sustainable future, but mainly for those who can afford it.

The synthetic, single-use nature of a pair of running shoes means that an average pair generates 30lb (13.6kg) of carbon dioxide. That's 'the equivalent to keeping a 100-watt light bulb on for one week' according to a 2013 MIT report, which identified the myriad manufacturing processes as a key contributor. Injection-moulding the sole features highly. With a focus on building a more sustainable future for running shoes, British brand Hylo Athletics increased the use of plant-based materials to reduce that figure to 20lb (8.63kg) without compromising either quality or performance for their flagship shoes.

Studies like this, as well as pressure from smaller, ideology-oriented challenger brands, even pushed Nike to advertise that they used a new foam in their 2024 Pegasus, which reduced the carbon footprint of the midsole by 'at least 43 per cent'. Every brand has their own carbon-plated shoes as a premium selection now, with Adidas offering a $500 option, and even high-street fast-fashion multinational Zara including a super shoe in their Athleticz range. The insatiable goal for speed has led to an addiction to the most unsustainable product possible – there is no second life for most running shoes. Can a more sustainable future catch on? Only time will tell, but the desire from many is there. Until then, we will pay the price, whatever it is.

OPPOSITE

More affordable options for running shoes could make scenes like this in Bangladesh less of a rarity.

RUN CLUBS

The question of how best to make friends has been bubbling under the surface for eternity, but when a pandemic slowly but surely rippled across the planet, life as we knew it changed beyond anything we'd either experienced or could have expected, and it brought our communities - and the difficulties in finding them - into razor-sharp focus.

For those living and working in cities around the world - over half the global population, and 80 per cent of people in the USA - there was a new normal. While service workers in America were hung out to dry with no pay at all as their places of work shuttered, the swathe of workers who would normally traipse into the office every morning suddenly had to grapple with the new dynamics of working from home. While the practical solutions of actually doing the white-collar work involved the relatively straightforward investment in a new desk and a chair to create a rudimentary home office set-up, the mental ramifications of adjusting to working in one's living space were much more complex. Losing those soupçons of small talk by the water cooler with a revolving cast of colleagues, coupled with the stress of a deadly novel virus circling the planet, led to many reassessing their priorities altogether.

Regardless, it had to be business as usual, rent had to be paid, but leaving our homes was prohibited beyond the government-mandated single daily hour of outdoor exercise. A newfound lack of a commute, however, meant that people also had an extra hour on their hands every day. Many chose to use that extra hour for their health and, as we know, the easiest and cheapest form of exercise is to simply open the door and go for a run. Those early days of the pandemic had a real 'make do and mend' mentality, so after pulling on any old pair of shorts and T-shirt, and a long rummage through a closet for that pair of running shoes you bought a few years ago, you ran. It felt good to be outside, shaking off the listlessness by using your body. When you saw someone else using their own hour of freedom to run, you may have felt a strange sense of familiarity. You may have waved at one another from afar the way runners do.

ABOVE

Bridgerunners in front of the Manhattan Bridge.

Research suggests that up to 30 per cent of runners in 2025 have begun running since the start of the pandemic, and a further 20 per cent run more now than they did before the pandemic. The big change is that 70 per cent of the new cohort of runners run for their health, compared to 20 per cent of runners pre-pandemic. The complementary statistic is that newer runners are less interested in competition, and instead look more at the social side of running: run clubs.

A survey by Running USA found the number of members of running clubs in the States has increased by 25 per cent since 2019. A Strava report identified that 78 per cent of runners in Jakarta, Indonesia, and 57 per cent of runners in Fortaleza, Brazil, ran with a group in 2024, and over a third of Los Angeles's social run clubs have sprouted up over the past three years, so this is a worldwide phenomenon, caused by a worldwide event.

BRIDGING THE GAP

The seeds of the latest wave of social running clans were sown a couple of decades prior, back in 2003 when Bridgerunners started running New York City's bridges from critically cool Lower Manhattan to Brooklyn and back again. In 2007, Run Dem Crew started kicking up their own fuss completely separately in equally hip east London. Eventually, the mercurial founders of these two crews met, and between Mike Saes and Charlie Dark, a movement was born.

Their run crews formed the idea of a new identity of runner. These were not people who readily identified with the post-collegiate running world found in American amateur running, nor had they ever followed a paper trail across the English countryside. That was so, so far from being their world. Their playground was the grimier parts of the big cities they call home. They were DJs, graffiti artists, your local friendly raconteurs, but they ran nonetheless, and they wanted to find the others like them who reflected modern pop culture while also running their streets.

OPPOSITE AND OVERLEAF

Shots of Bridgerunners and Girls Run NYC.

BROADWAY
HOWARD ST
WAY
ONE WAY

69—71
WARNING
BRIDGERUNNERS
New York City

Support
Women

Over the next five years, they would go on to find similar run crews based in inner cities across Europe and America, and then further around the world. Late one night, Bridgerunners and Run Dem Crew concocted the idea of Bridge The Gap, where they created events around the globe, bringing together and celebrating the small but incredibly connected Rolodex of like-minded urban running crews like NBRO from Copenhagen, Berlin Braves, Paris Running Club and Patta in Amsterdam. Every time they converged upon a city from their corners of the world, they would emerge from the airport dressed in matching jackets, like they were a band. Jessie Zapo, who was one of the main organizers, explains how they would 'touch down, put our stuff in the apartment, then we were clubbing that first night with all the people from all these other cities. The energy was electric.' This would prove to be the first era of social run crews' longest-lasting legacy – one that has gone on to inspire future generations of run clubs tens of thousands of miles further afield.

The concept of running clubs is nothing new, of course. While clubs such as the New York Pioneer Club formed in 1936 have been around since before World War II, it was clubs like Prospect Park Track Club and Central Park Track Club, which were started in the 1970s, and have endured for over half a century. Another of the earliest clubs still running cross-country is the Thames Hare and Hounds, which formed in London in 1868. Back in 19th-century England, practising sports as competition during leisure time was the preserve of the 'gentleman amateur'. With the art of cross-country running born from the stuffy boys' school system, it was a fast run through the woods reserved for the best educated in the country. The UK still excels in this type of athletic club for serious amateur runners, which provide low-cost competition and community. You'll see each club's unique singlet in among the front-runners at the London Marathon, on the starting line at parkruns around the country, and dotted around at social running clubs' meet-ups as well.

One of the common reasons given for not enjoying the traditional athletics club experience in the UK is that they can often seem a little old-fashioned. However, while these new, more social run crews might have started out as

OPPOSITE

Shots of Bridgerunners and Girls Run NYC.

OVERLEAF

Mile Style crew members relaxing after Take The Bridge.

MILE
STYLE
68
STYLE
66

SMART
Family Day Care
KIDS FROM 6 WEEKS
TO 12 YEARS OLD
NIÑOS DESDE 6 SEMANAS
A 12 AÑOS
226 Kimberly Pl Bronx, NY 10463
718-884-2375
STYLE
1

distinct from the established athletics clubs, by congregating at a watering hole instead of a track or clubhouse, slowly but surely they have added structure and desire to their club cultures. As members improved as runners, they wanted to run races. A marathon is the natural progression, and so they picked up training plans, added track workouts and long runs to the weekly schedule, and maybe even joined those stuffy, old-fashioned clubs. They may have emerged from left field, but ultimately some became just another option for runners looking to improve themselves. That journey was the conduit to Jessie Zapo getting her coaching qualification and then leaving her decade-long tenure as a captain in Bridgerunners to first form Black Roses, which had a deep focus on performance training, and then brought that mindset with her when forming one of New York's first women-only clubs, Girls Run NYC.

In the same way, many of the new running clubs from the past quarter of a century act as grassroots communities that build a meeting point for a splinter of society. There are women-only clubs and LGBTQIA+-friendly communities like Frontrunners, clubs for South Asians like Masala Milers in New York or Sikhs In The City in London, there's Black Men Run, which is a national organization of clubs across the United States whose goal is to get more Black men into the sport, and so many more. They all exist to support those marginalized groups of people who might not otherwise see themselves represented in the running world.

Run clubs have been a bold new conduit to expanding social representation within the sport, and, as a result, more people are running. As that happens, there will be greater numbers available to form these groups, so the make-up of the groups will diversify from the purity of just running for competition, or for friendship. We will see more and more reasons for people to join together and run. There's a thought that, increasingly, there will be a focus to involve secondary activities, whether that's layering another exercise in terms of adding HIIT or cycling, or a purely social element such as a speed dating event.

Finding a romantic partner is one of the most natural things in the world, after all, and if you're in the same place and doing the same thing as someone you're

OPPOSITE

Ted Corbitt from the New York Pioneers Club competing in the 1975 New York City Marathon.

NEW YORK
6

attracted to, you've already got two things in common. People joining a social event to find love is a tale as old as time. The Boston Barleyhoppers are a great example from the 1970s as they pulled up to 300 runners to the Bull & Finch pub – the setting for classic sitcom *Cheers* – before running through the Massachusetts capital. Twenty-two marriages came from the Barleyhoppers. Simpler times, perhaps, but founder Eddie Doyle has one hell of a legacy.

And if there can be a time-efficient global network to find love via running, who says no? It might even help preserve the purity of those non-dating clubs.

A PLACE TO MAKE FRIENDS AND INFLUENCE PEOPLE

The concept of third places was coined by Ray Oldenburg in his 1989 book, *The Great Good Place*. While a first place is your home, and a second place is where you work, a third place is neutral ground away from responsibilities, where you can relax and converse with strangers in an informal situation, often in the same neighbourhood as either home or work.

These third places might take the form of a coffee shop, bar or restaurant, a library, gym or dog park. Community centres and churches are also popular third places. Many of these locations often hit the headlines for disappearing from neighbourhoods for a variety of reasons, including more online communication and the decline of small businesses in favour of corporate chains. When we also consider the loss of a second place for those thrust into their new working life in a home office, third places become even more crucial.

You may also notice that all of these examples have a low financial barrier, and that is essential for accessibility. These casual, low-cost interactions were once easy to take for granted, but when they became a little more difficult to come by, people sprang into action. Run clubs, by and large, are free, and there was an explosion of social running clubs around the world, which have given people a place to form real new relationships.

In his 2000 book, *Bowling Alone*, American political scientist Robert Putnam outlines how America's social capital has been in decline since the 1950s through a combination of an ever-growing distrust of government and a more car-dependent, suburbanized population, as well as demographic changes.

Human nature dictates that socializing and community building are still a priority for all. Oldenburg states that third places are essential for people to foster a sense of belonging, which strengthens communities as well as the well-being of individuals.

The title of Putnam's book comes from his observation that while the number of people bowling had increased over the previous two decades, the number of people bowling in leagues had decreased. Even though we know that no man is an island, people were increasingly bowling alone or in pairs – definitely not within an established community, anyway. Can running with your friends be the answer to the global epidemic of loneliness?

Consider the intimacy of running with a friend versus running with a stranger. We experience intimacy in so many different ways throughout our lives, and even within a day. While the intimacy within a couple is often the first thing that comes to mind, consider the more pedestrian occurrence of feeding someone or of helping someone dress themselves. Think about the level of care and trust that requires. It's what a parent does for their child. It's what the closest of friends would do for you when you need it most. For me, intimacy is sharing a vulnerable moment with someone else and, for me, that intimacy is key to the beauty of running.

When runners are asked to pinpoint what it is about running that we love so much, both mental and physical health are near the top of the list. Next we might talk about enjoying the runner's high or being outside, in nature. The thrill of seeing how far and how fast our bodies can take us can often be cited. All of these things take on a different nature when shared with someone else. Finding enjoyment, peace or our limits becomes a deeper experience when we do them with others.

On an individual level, there's an intimacy to understanding your body more fully as you move through your running journey, but there's also an intimacy to trusting your physical and mental health to a coach and the training plan they draw up for your race-specific goals. You trust that they understand your body's capability and possibilities even better than you do. You're trusting that they can bring the best out of you. Whether you succeed or not, you're sharing that moment with another person.

RUN CREW
THE IDEA O
A NEW IDE
OF RUNNE

S FORMED
OF

In a run club, however, when you can finally pause at the end of the group run, gasping for breath, nobody cares how dishevelled and sweaty you look. After a serious workout, you might be full of emotion – whether that's satisfaction, frustration, pain or elation – and, again, you're sharing that moment with those around you. It's a moment that you might not normally think to share, but you're already standing among others just like you. The bond has already been created in silence, just by being there together in that moment.

Think about the fellow run-clubber who's waiting with purpose on the edges of a race to hand you a fresh bottle of electrolytes. Or the ones waiting for you at the end, willing you over the finish line to celebrate. Consider the intimacy with those in your life who understand the needs at the core of your being. Those are immediate and unbreakable bonds.

When the bar that I met my wife in closed down, the owner said in an interview that the thing he missed the most were the people who he saw every day, or every week, but only ever knew their first name, but that was enough to say hello to and have a friendly conversation with. I knew exactly what he was talking about because I have run-club friends who I've known for years and see every week, but have never had their phone number. It's that matter of trust again. When you know that you'll see them again at the same time in the same place, the knowledge that you can continue your conversation the following week is a beautifully comfortable act.

It's all these layers of intimacy, perhaps, that make runners want to share their sport with their nearest and dearest non-runners. This explains why this intimacy builds community so easily and so strongly, and why we are so proud and protective of the communal spaces that we've created for us to be vulnerable in.

Engaging in real community is a bold step towards happiness. When that community bands together in times of crisis, for instance, incredibly strong bonds can be formed in record time. During the Los Angeles wildfires of January 2025, run clubs from across the city came together in a beautiful act of mutual aid. Koreatown Run Club commandeered a warehouse to package up and then hand-deliver hundreds of boxes of supplies to affected residents; members of Eagle Rock Run Club were right there at ground zero helping with the clean-up; and Silver Lake Track Club organized an unsanctioned relay over the 30 miles (50km) between Altadena and the Pacific Palisades that raised over $50,000 for wildfire-related causes.

If you're wondering why run clubs are so special, there is your evidence starter pack.

ABOVE

Tina, a member of Run Dem Crew competes in a race.

Mike Saes

Bridgerunners NYC

It was 2003 when Mike Saes truly began his love affair with running over the bridges of New York. Before that, he was running through necessity – away from the cops. Over 20 years later, the mercurial founder of Bridgerunners NYC is still exploring his city, running through all five boroughs, and he'll take as many people with him as he can.

WHAT DID BRIDGERUNNERS CHANGE ABOUT RUNNING CULTURE?

I think running before us was boring. It was running around the park to get it over with. Now it's about exploration and adventure, seeing and learning, because when you're looking at things, not looking at the time on the treadmill or your watch, you just run 8 miles without even thinking about it. Our mindset is we're going to make the world a better place above everything else. We have this mobile meditation, where we can just run for 5 miles. It's healing for us to run, and all I'm doing is providing roots and culture to make that healing pleasurable.

WHAT HAPPENS WHEN YOUR RUN CREW ISN'T SERVING THE NEEDS OF ALL ITS MEMBERS?

The movement is about more crews. Wherever there's a void, fill it with love and leadership. Make sure that you're training the next captain to do the same. Especially more female captains and leaders. I don't mean just female crews – I mean female captains. If you've been coming to Bridgerunners for six months, I expect you to be able to start your own crew. It doesn't have to be a carbon copy of Bridgerunners, it could just fill the void because there's a lot

of voids, and leadership is needed. We've trained you to become a leader. That's the whole point.

WHAT IS THE LEGACY OF MODERN RUNNING CLUBS

Bridgerunners' legacy is that we did it for the right reasons. We didn't do it to be cool. We were already cool. But this is not a trend. This is a lifestyle. From what I hear, it's changed a lot of lives for the better. I know I'm a lot better. If every Wednesday for the last 21 years I got with my graffiti friends and wrote in black books and smoked weed, I don't think I would be as healthy as I am right now. I chose to use my Wednesday to be healthy. Crew culture is here to stay for ever and ever.

A NEW WAVE OF CONSUMERISM

'Running is the new streetwear,' cries one headline. Another tells you, 'The pavement can be your runway!' You look around your run club and there might be a bunch of sullen, androgynous faces wrapped in bug-eyed sunglasses, and they're all decked out in starkly monochrome attire. Are they going to a concert? Are they *in* the band?? But then you see them run effortlessly down the street, and you realize that they just really care about how they *look* when they're running.

The idea of running apparel as something more than pure performance gear is not completely new - look at Adidas's 20-plus-year relationship with Yohji Yamamoto and his Y-3 brand, for instance - but the confluence of fashion and running is increasingly visible. Just as the 1970s running boom was in part inspired by the rise of streetwear in youth fashion as rebellious young people sought to emulate and aspire to the looks of their sporting heroes, something similar is happening in today's influencer-rich world of pop culture. Runners have always readily identified as nerds about their running and, as the sport has grown, the spectrum of nerdiness has expanded to include people who care deeply about other subcultures, including fashion.

This new trend may have been popularized by a mood board first envisioned in a New York nightclub in 2003, when Mike Saes of Bridgerunners bumped into an acquaintance who worked at Wieden+Kennedy, Nike's advertising agency. The New York run crew were notorious for running in their regular street clothes. Air Force Ones and basketball shorts were the order of the day, and

OPPOSITE AND OVERLEAF

Shots from running brand Soar.

PACE

that effortless street style proved attractive to Nike, who ended up supporting Bridgerunners to help build the community through events as well as using the crew's inimitable style in numerous campaigns to promote running as a sport. Since then, the appearance of runners has moved further and further away from functional garments, towards clothes that express ideas and personality.

Take Paris Fashion Week, for instance. Running brands have long shown their wares at fashion shows in New York, London and further afield, but with founder Brice Partouche's background in denim and menswear, French self-professed running cult Satisfy put on their own show, and so did Hermanos Koumori, another former denim and menswear brand from Mexico that has pivoted completely to high-end performance running apparel. While a new batch of brands that blend performance with bleeding-edge design like Soar, Norda and Unna were also present in the capital of haute couture, so were more traditional brands, like Brooks and Merrell, who you'd be forgiven for associating slightly less with high fashion. Running was represented across the spectrum, and the idea of running as a subculture of fashion that's worthy of being enmeshed within the wider fashion world was promoted with glorious fervour. It felt like runners were legitimate outsiders in the fashion space.

While these fashion-focused brands are boldly redefining how we consume our sport, and the creativity is hugely exciting, do these spaces check the boxes of accessibility or sustainability? Whether it's your intention or not, clothes have always been the easiest way to send an instant, visual message to everyone around you. You can wear a band shirt to display your taste in music, or a three-piece suit to cosplay as a business leader or wedding guest. A kaftan or kimono can signal what country you're from, and a $200 singlet will outline your spending power in one glance.

Within running, with its reputation as the most egalitarian and democratic of physical pursuits, the idea of fashion is a curious one. Within Marxism, the fashion world is sunken into the deepest ideas of capitalist production – global labour exploitation – thus exacerbating economic inequalities in society. If you're wearing last season's clothes, you can forget about hanging out with the

OPPOSITE

The inimitable Steve Prefontaine.

cool kids. Yes, the primitive social dynamics of our teenage years are rearing their ugly heads once more, but this time in our running world. It's the bourgeoisie versus the proletariat; the rich kids wearing $200 shorts, posturing in front of those on a more meagre budget. If we know that the fashion world has long hawked ideas that have come from the streets before reformatting and reappropriating them into luxury goods, fashion in running is absolutely no different. If your shirt has holes in, is it a garment you've lovingly worn for 20 years, or have those holes been digitally heat-mapped? Either way, it's not about running fast – it's about looking like you can.

'Some people create with words or with music or with a brush and paints. I like to make something beautiful when I run. I like to make people stop and say, "I've never seen anyone run like that before." It's more than just a race, it's a style. It's doing something better than anyone else. It's being creative.' So said the legendary Steve Prefontaine, giving his views on how to use your aura to look beautiful while running.

How we engage with that side of running is crucial. While it's true that with increasing numbers of runners, it is inevitable there will be an increasing number of niches, including an incredibly visible one for those interested in haute fashion, the majority of runners engage more readily with performance apparel that suits their budgets. Part of that budgeting is living sustainably, and for that we can lean on the old adage of 'Reduce, Reuse, Recycle'.

We do live and take part in a world based on pure capitalism, though, and some are of the mindset that there is no ethical consumption at all under capitalism – so how do we make the best of it while we wait for the prevailing economic structure of the planet to be overthrown for a gentler, more harmonious system? There's the argument that luxury goods, though expensive, will last longer. Many of the new breed of running apparel brands focus on the higher quality of their clothing, backing it up with lifetime guarantees. So, buying fewer items is a start, but buying garments made from natural fibres, which will biodegrade in months and years rather than the centuries that synthetic materials take to break down in landfill, is a great way to purchase with a little more thought. Wearing those clothes in non-athletic arenas would give them a secondary purpose, halving their price-per-wear value, which makes sense considering how much new gear can cost.

If $1,000 outfits are the new normal, however, PYNRS is a fantastic example of what the future of the sport can look like. After Sid Baptista found running, he brought running back to the people in his 'super-segregated' hometown of Dorchester, Boston, in the form of Pioneers Run Crew. He started by building a community, and then identified the need for clothing that represents that community, so included them in the creation of the first Black-owned performance running apparel brand in the USA.

'It's for the people, so we've allowed people to invest in it,' Baptista explains. 'It's directly crowdfunded, allowing them to share in some of the revenue. It's about creating something that's a voice, a reflection, an outlet, a representation. [If we] give our culture over to these brands, we're never going to own anything. We already do this, so let's put a company in front of it. Something that's really owned by the culture.'

When there is the question of the ethics of leveraging a community for commerce, this is how to do it. By building a foundation of disenfranchised runners who firstly want quality garments that represent them, but also want it to come from within, they will all win together. If we return to the Marxist viewpoint that culture is used to segregate society and that dominant cultures can be challenged over time, there is a way for the grassroots of running to reclaim the streets that they built in the first place.

CREAM AND TWO SUGARS, PLEASE

A major knock-on effect of the proliferation of this new wave of running apparel brands is that they have needed a suitable place to sell them. While selling online, direct to the consumer, works incredibly well for limited releases and low budgets, flagship stores are an expensive investment, even if they are a wonderful advertisement of everything a brand singularly represents. It also feels wrong placing these beautifully designed garments in existing, traditional running stores that are often piled high with cardboard boxes, with circular rails that are packed close together with every possible piece of running apparel hanging from them. You know the ones.

The prototype of the new wave of boutique running stores may have been NikeTown in London's West End. It took up a whole corner of Oxford Circus, at the intersection of Oxford Street and Regent Street, when it opened in 1999,

THE CONF
FASHION &
IS INCREA
VISIBLE

LUENCE OF
RUNNING
SINGLY

and while the six-floor celebration of the Swoosh was the opposite of an off-the-beaten-path boutique, the aesthetic and direction was clear. Come in, immerse yourself in the brand, shop quietly and carefully. Maybe you'll leave with a bag tastefully emblazoned with the logo.

Even though Nike are the godfathers of modern running, having launched the major part of their footwear brand off Steve Prefontaine wearing the still-distinctive waffle sole created by Bill Bowerman in 1972, when NikeTown opened, running was on the back burner. It was tucked away up many flights of escalators, but you could still try on all of their latest technical gear at your leisure. It wicked the sweat off your body in record time, and supported your arches better than the rest, and you could see it for yourself inside of a beautifully designed monument to Nike. It felt special.

Another landmark moment was the bright, airy and fun Tracksmith pop-up at the 2014 Boston Marathon on Newbury Street. That road is now filled with similarly styled pop-up stores from every brand under the sun every April. Tracksmith developed and executed a new concept for a bright, spacious running boutique where single items of their preppy, collegiate running apparel were showcased on shelves, rather than crammed together tight on racks. Bandit, too, has a beautifully minimalist store in Manhattan, New York, that shares space with a coffee shop and two enormous speakers. The idea is that running is just part of your lifestyle. You enjoy the finer things in life, so why not these high-quality running clothes as well?

Neither brand launched with shoes. Clothes only. Both can be found in the new wave of multi-brand running stores, for which shoes do form the backbone of their income. These stores are an alternative rather than a replacement. Their customers share a love of running with the previous generation of runners, but sometimes you wouldn't know it to look at them. These places celebrate an esoteric idea of the latest incarnation of running culture, which melds performance, lifestyle and community all at the same time.

OPPOSITE

The full range of Janji apparel.

OVERLEAF

PYNRS apparel being put through its paces.

PYNRS

PYNRS

They borrow from the idea of the third-wave coffee shops, which are bright and spacious, with a stark, minimalist aesthetic that evokes Japanese or Scandinavian design philosophies, with local artwork for sale on the walls and little design flourishes intended to convey the deeper thought that's been put into architecting the space. As the coffee shops highlight the unique qualities and flavours of the coffee itself, with a focus on artisanal, small-batch beans, the third wave of multi-brand running stores mimics those ideals.

Just as those coffee shops encourage and enjoy increased education around harvesting more sustainably sourced beans, these brands and retailers extol the virtues of the higher-quality materials and manufacturing that go into boutique brands. Traditional running stores service their locale in much the same way a local London greasy spoon café does: dependable with no frills. You get an expert opinion on your gait analysis for a new pair of shoes from one, and a perfectly cooked bacon sandwich from the other.

A huge change in attitude for today's coffee shops is how they defy being labelled as pure retail outlets because they encourage the formation of community by allowing customers to stay there and work or read a book, with less onus on buying coffee after coffee to justify their stay. Existing running stores have long been pillars of the community, but the new ones make that a central tenet. Building these communities isn't a brazen act of market capture, of course. There is a real intent to create third-place hubs, just as run clubs do, in order to allow the local running community to blossom and thrive.

The relationship is ultimately between a running store owner and a customer, so the community that is built isn't traditional or fully reciprocal – it's more transactional. We have a pure version of a running community in the form of clubs and crews, after all. When the relationship is understood by both parties, however, they can begin to create the correct partnership, which involves the major recipient adding a greater amount of value to the community. Then they can become exciting places to make new, fast friends.

OPPOSITE

Satisfy shorts passing the sweat test.

SATISFY

ABOVE

Tracksmith gear in its natural environment.

Metta Running House in Mexico City, for instance, has a full cafe and showers, allowing runners to integrate their run into their day a little more naturally, and Interval in Edinburgh hosts a subsidized, coached weekly track night, improving accessibility to speed workouts. Renegade in Oakland, California, regularly shines a light on local minority-owned run clubs in events, while Knees Up in London hosts fashion shows and panels. Running Wylder is a woman-owned store in the heart of San Francisco, and the space feels delightfully unique: less polished concrete and more carefully curated local products. It's exactly what we want from a modern, neighbourhood running store.

First, though, was Distance Athletics in Lyon, France, which opened in 2018. It was a beautiful concept store: a boutique; the blueprint. Now, with four stores around the world, the tiny original store blended a highly curated lifestyle boutique with quality garments and essential footwear. The idea is to showcase the owner's ideas in a way that someone trusts their level of curation to become more than just a customer, just like the local art you see in third-wave coffee shops. It's something different, and more thoughtful.

Stepping into these spaces can transform a mindset from pure performance or utilitarian purchasing into considering one's visual identity, and many are coming to understand that looking good is the first step in feeling the freedom of running fast. This might be a more elevated experience than your parents' local running store, but one way or another the nerdiness reigns supreme nonetheless.

Matt Taylor

Founder of Tracksmith

From blogging about the stories of college runners, by way of telling Usain Bolt and the Kenyan marathoners' stories, to a multimillion-dollar premium running apparel brand, Matt Taylor has had a singular vision for how he wanted the sport of running to be seen. Founding Tracksmith under a glorious shroud of Americana-based nostalgia was the culmination of a life's work.

AT WHAT POINT IN YOUR CAREER DID YOU THINK ABOUT STARTING TRACKSMITH?

The entire premise of my life, from a career perspective, has been this insatiable desire to change the way that running is perceived, and the only way to change the way it's perceived is to change the way it's presented. At 20-something years old, I was naïve to think I was going to do that. I was average or below average in [writing, photography and filmmaking] individually, but I was really the only person creating content like that back then.

WAS THERE A DEFINING MOMENT THAT MADE YOU WANT TO CREATE SOMETHING DIFFERENT?

There was a particular story in 1995 or 1996 in Runner's World about an athlete named Marc Davis. He was a steeplechaser for the US and made the Olympics in 1996, and he was a little bit of the bad boy in running, if there could be such a thing in distance running in the nineties. I was reading ESPN the magazine and Sports Illustrated at the time, and what's crazy is that the article on this guy was photographed and written in a way that had never been done in a running magazine. To me, that was a little bit of the kernel. You never just wake up one day and everything's there. You piece these things together over time.

What I found out recently is that article was written for GQ as a profile leading into the Olympics, but I guess GQ didn't want to run it, and last minute it got sold to Runner's World. Now that makes total sense because it is the type of article I would have expected in a GQ or Rolling Stone or something of that era.

CAN YOU EXPLAIN THE TRACKSMITH IN-STORE EXPERIENCE?

There is still a customer that wants to touch and feel the product. You look at these stores, and compared to what we grew up with – boxes stacked to the ceiling; clothes on rounders, packed so tight you need to use your muscles to pull two shirts apart – [it's] a much more curated and considered presentation.

In 2014, we did our first pop-up at the Boston Marathon. I just happened to be walking down Newbury Street and saw this for lease sign, and thought, 'Maybe we could get lucky and convince the landlord to let us take it for one week.' And we did, spending the same amount of money as a ten-by-ten booth at the expo, and we were able to present it in the way that we wanted. That was a pivotal moment in the brand's history. It was a lightbulb moment that there was something there. Ten years later, and now every brand is on Newbury Street, doing exactly the same thing.

IS RUNNING THE NEW SKATEBOARDING?

There is a faction of running that is the new skateboarding, but running is so broad. The vast majority of people have done it in their life. With that comes hundreds of millions of opinions of what running is and what it should be. Not many people question what skateboarding is or what it should be. Skateboarding as a culture is pretty monogamous. When you look at running, every cohort is represented. It's the one true melting-pot sport.

THE FEMALE EXPERIENCE

They say that you never forget your first, and it's true: they're indelible memories. Your first kiss, cozied up in the corner at a house party. The first band you just couldn't stop listening to – you still listen to them, in fact. The first time you truly understood what violence against women meant. That was in February 2003. I wasn't yet 20 years old when I heard about the shocking murder of American artist Margaret Muller as she was jogging in east London. My side of London.

The attack struck thunderously across the newswires, and still resonates deeply with me on so many levels. I had artist friends who lived a stone's throw from where she was killed in Hackney. Those neighbourhoods started to look different to us from that day. The shadows held more menace even though the attack took place in broad daylight. Victoria Park is now a bustling location for so many runners, including London's premier run club, Your Friendly Runners, whose home base café, Knees Up, is less than a mile from where Margaret's body was found.

Over 20 years later, Margaret Muller's murder is still unsolved – there was a fresh appeal for information in 2023 – and I think about her every time another woman is attacked. Running or not. So what's changed in that time? Either not a lot or so much, depending on how you want to look at it.

A lot of the headline items, like reproductive rights and equal pay, were passed in the second wave of feminism in the 1970s. Society took until not long before that to catch up with the science of the early 20th century. The science in question was about a woman's uterus falling out during competitive running.

OPPOSITE

Kathrine Switzer being wrestled from the Boston Marathon course in 1967.

225
261
295

Yes, it seems absurd to read that right now, but we're only 50 years removed from enough people still thinking that to be true to need to pass Title IX legislation (1972) in the United States, which ensured by law that girls would have access to sports in publicly funded schools.

For instance, women were not allowed to run the Boston Marathon back in 1966 when Bobbi Gibb bandited the course by jumping out from behind a bush at the start, or the following year when race official Jock Semple attempted to wrestle Kathrine Switzer (registered as KV Switzer) from the course. So when Title IX was passed, and then a couple of years later, in 1974, women were allowed to have a credit card, it felt like good progress. It felt like we were living in a real society. Switzer continued working hard after that marathon to revolutionize women's sports, driving the change to the rule at the Boston Marathon so women could enter from 1972, as well as campaigning for the women's marathon to be an Olympic event.

It took another three years for a similar rule to be implemented in the UK, where women were barred from competing in races over 6km (3.73 miles) until April 1975. This was all before the jogging boom of the 1970s, so while it could seem like a very conservative thing to ban women from doing, the governing body, the Women's Amateur Athletic Association, outlined in their initial objectives in 1922 that their primary goal was to protect the few women who wanted to compete. They wanted separate changing facilities, for example, to help protect women from objectification when they wore competition clothing. Beyond the WAAA, British women had no voice in the media or in other areas of athletics legislation, so progress was slow, but it was progress nonetheless.

Cut to 2014 in New York, and we're 40 years removed from those sea changes and into the fourth wave of feminism. We're also a decade into the new urban running club scene, which is welcoming of women and supportive spaces, but is ultimately created and held by men. Jessie Zapo was a veteran leader of Bridgerunnners at this point, but she 'could count women coaches in running

OPPOSITE

Girls Run NYC member.

GIRLS RUN NYC

PROGRESS
SLOW, BUT
PROGRESS
NONETHEL

WAS

IT WAS

ESS

on two hands'. Despite living, working and running in New York – one of the most forward-thinking cities in the world – there were no all-women groups, so she created Girls Run NYC, and inspired generations of female runners around the world.

In May 2019, Allyson Felix, one of the USA's most decorated Olympians, spoke to Congress about the dire state of Black maternal health – a mortality crisis that persists to this day due to bias – that she experienced first-hand after a difficult pregnancy that culminated in an emergency caesarean. This advocacy for mothers was extended to Nike's poor treatment of its athletes. Felix standing up for women to the highest level of government helped to rally other elite female athletes who had been wronged by the way Nike's sponsorship deals were constructed. Nike offered Felix a 70 per cent reduction in her contract after she informed them of her plans to start a family.

Earlier that week, another American Olympic medallist, Alysia Montaño, had flipped the script on Nike's 'Dream Crazier' slogan in an op-ed in the *New York Times*, and the story went viral.

That *NYT* op-ed also featured fellow Nike elite athlete Kara Goucher, who held off announcing her pregnancy so that Nike could announce it on Mother's Day. Once Goucher gave birth, however, Nike told her that she wouldn't get any more money until she started formally racing again, so Goucher was in training one week after childbirth. She later suffered chronic hip injuries after racing the Boston Marathon just seven months after becoming a mother. This is interesting to consider because scientists have calculated that the most energy a human can burn is 2.5 times the basal metabolic rate, during a marathon, for instance. A pregnant woman, however, burns 2.2 times her BMR for the entirety of her 40-week gestation. As more scientific research like this is done in areas like pregnancy, periods and fuelling, we can move forward with more definition, allowing more women to participate in sports.

The result of Felix and Montaño's public work was Nike agreeing a new maternity policy that protects and guarantees all sponsored athletes' pay for 18 months

OPPOSITE

Alysia Montaño waves to the crowd at the US Track and Field Championships in 2017 while five months pregnant.

8
UCS
7
UCS
4
8
MARTINEZ

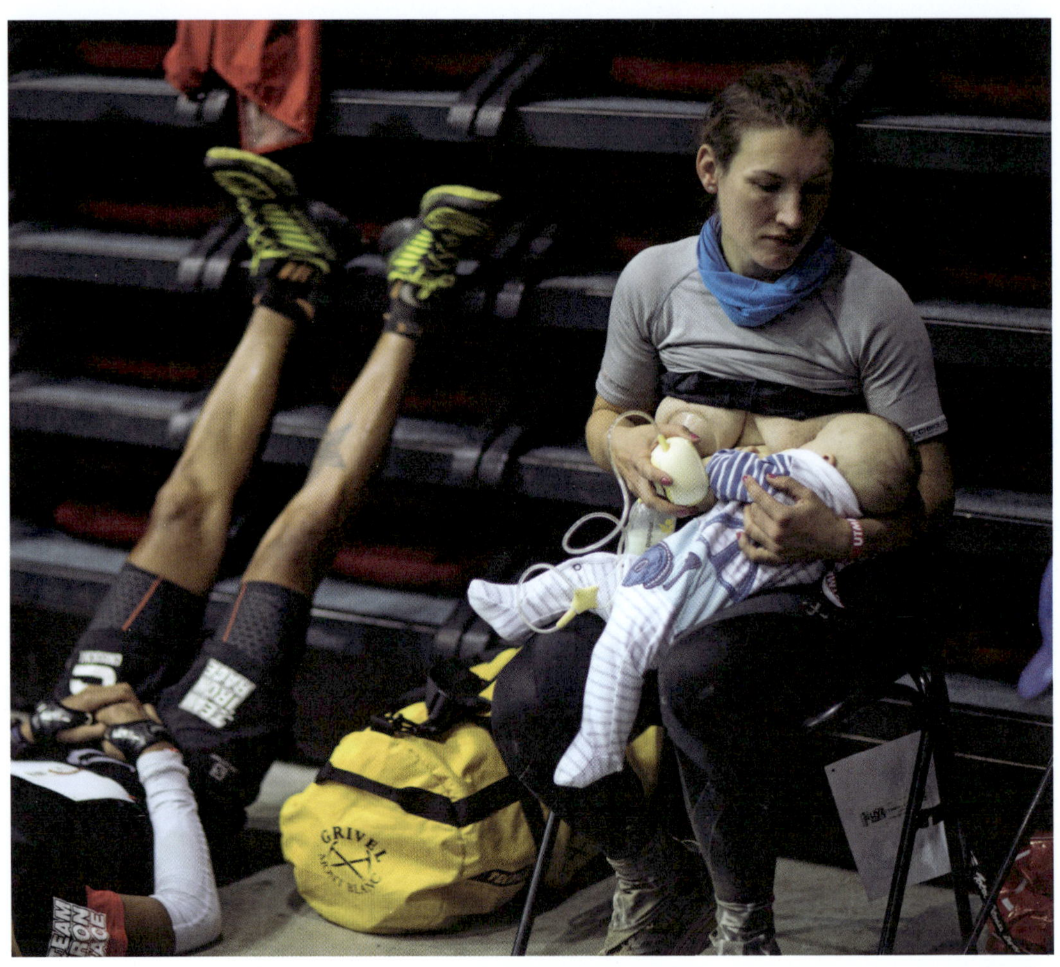

ABOVE

Sophie Power breastfeeding her baby while racing the UTMB in 2018.

around their pregnancies. Following Nike's lead, several other companies implemented similar protections for pregnant athletes. From an admittedly high-profile position within running, real change was effected within multiple corporations across all sports.

Another place where increased gender parity is very much being encouraged is on the trails, where as many as 63 per cent of trail runners are men. Insider reports suggest that trail running is a place that is welcoming to all, but is just lacking equal representation across both gender and race. Acknowledging the reasons, however, is important, and while safety concerns abound, there are several organizations and people trying to break the hegemony.

Dora Atim, for instance, founded Ultra Black Running to help Black women and non-binary people in London enjoy trail running, after being stopped and questioned while running during a brief but significant moment of living outside of her cosmopolitan home of London. It was an experience that prompted Dora to question who has access to running in these spaces, and why. That led to her organizing runs in the English capital's gloriously green heaths, parks and forests for her people.

Another organization directly working to achieve a better race experience for women is SheRACES, which was formed by British ultrarunner Sophie Power after she achieved notoriety by being photographed while breastfeeding her three-month-old baby at the UTMB. She wanted to defer her place that year, but the race organizers only allowed deferrals for injury – they classified pregnancy and young motherhood as a choice. After that photograph went viral, Power was contacted by enough race organizers to know that something had to be done, and that she was going to be the one to do it, so she set about formulating some guidelines that helped fill the gap in knowledge that those race organizers were suffering from, with a goal of encouraging more female race applicants and participants. The suggestions include more inclusive imagery, softer language used to describe the race, enhanced safety for longer races that go through the night, more generous cut-off times to aid those at the back of the pack, improved changing facilities and toilets, more information to aid planning for the race, equalizing prize money and coverage, and fairer deferral policies, of course.

The London Marathon is the highest-profile race to have adopted the SheRACES guidelines and they achieved parity between male and female ballot entrants by focusing their messaging on back-of-the-pack runners, giving women more confidence to enter races, knowing there is no cut-off time and that they will be supported and celebrated for the entirety of their run. It's a forward-thinking move from the London Marathon as they received a record number of ballot entries for 2026 – a 30 per cent increase from the previous year. The marathon also allows deferral following pregnancy for up to three years, but they only keep the spot warm. The athlete still has to pay all the race fees every year they defer.

Aside from making that marathon an incredibly expensive run, it's another part of the fitness gap, where women get less exercise than men. Headline-grabbing women like Jasmin Paris and Sophie Power, who do amazing things, help to paper over these particular societal cracks. The US government's Centres for Disease Control and Prevention reports that while just 28.3 per cent of American men meet physical activity guidelines for both aerobic and muscle-strengthening activities, the number for women is only 20.4 per cent. Whether it's the disproportionate amount of labour that women have to perform, the emotional or domestic labour while raising a family, or societal norms that dictate that women look after everyone else first or exercise for weight loss rather than for joy, the data tells the story.

WHAT WOMEN HAVE TO THINK ABOUT WHEN THEY THINK ABOUT RUNNING

Away from competitive racing or running the trails, running in cities as a woman poses a sadly familiar set of problems that takes a whole new level of thought. While women no longer need to dress up as a man to run a marathon, they still have to deal with being cat-called, followed and attacked. Nine out of ten women worry about running alone, so this means that they have to put serious extra thought into finding a safe route that is well lit and more likely to have other pedestrians, or finding a group to run with and adjusting their schedule to fit in with the group. If they do decide to run alone, consideration might go into what they're going to wear so as not to attract unwanted attention, and making sure the Find My Friends app is up and running on their phone. It's extra labour that men are far less likely to have to perform.

If we understand the concept of having a certain bandwidth of mind where you can make 10,000 high-quality decisions in a day, it begins to make more sense. It's why the late Steve Jobs and now Mark Zuckerberg wear the same clothes every day. Removing that decision reserves that extra jot of brain power for the most important decisions during the day. I will posit that having to think about one's safety while running in a civilized society is not a reasonable use of a high-quality decision.

The knock-on effects of this extra mental labour for women is tangible. Studies have shown that people who are more tired than average, in this case due to a higher than average number of subconscious decisions being made per day, will have less brain power to invest in decision-making, which in turn leads to less deep thought, which ultimately leads to making suboptimal choices and lowering performance. Running becomes a more strenuous act. The extra mental load that women take on when planning and running a route through the city literally impairs their athletic performance. Women are exhausted, and it strips the joy from their running practice.

Henri Lefebvre's concepts of inclusive social and public spaces are just as relevant over 50 years after they were thought up by the Frenchman in the 1970s. His ideas that the built environment is not just a physical space, but is inherently social and political, can be transposed to running. Running is social. Running is political. As you run through a public space, you are an icon of everything that you are and believe in. One of Lefebvre's most famous ideas, and maybe his most popular, is that urban space should be reclaimed by the people, for it is they who deserve to benefit from the places in which they live; that the people should be deeply involved in the decision-making for the city. It's the idea of creating a city for the people who are actually using it.

Currently, cities are overwhelmingly created by white men: 62 per cent of architects in the USA are white men, but progress is being made as 9 per cent of new architects in the States are Asian women, so maybe another sea change of progress is coming. Change is difficult, of course, because it can be a question of yielding power - something that doesn't happen lightly - but if we frame it economically, studies have indicated that companies with more diverse and inclusive workforces make better decisions 85 per cent of the time, and are 35 per cent more likely to outperform their peers. The lessons are right there to be learned. We can create better cities if we have a more diverse input.

OBIRI
LIMO
SCOTT
SISSON
NEW YORK MINI 10K

Progress, however, is neither linear nor something that can be completed and there will likely always be more questions than answers. How can we solve the dearth of women running in their thirties? How can we make sport more accessible around the world? How can we truly celebrate a world record time if the fastest woman in the world has to spend her time doing an unfair proportion of the emotional labour in the home?

Everyone who helps to push running culture forward for women does incredibly important work. Just as Kathrine Switzer had her coach and boyfriend in her corner as she blazed a trail through the Boston Marathon, and Jessie Zapo had Mike Saes and the rest of the Bridgerunners in hers when she launched Girls Run NYC, strong, correct-thinking allies are necessary for true progress to occur. Everyone who's watching women's sports will always want to see the best athletes performing to the maximum of their abilities.

The current uptick in runners is largely fuelled by Gen Z women taking up running, so it feels more possible than ever to move the needle in mainstream culture by affecting and enacting change within the niche of running. For instance, if you're prone to saying that all you need to go for a run is a good pair of shoes, consider adding a good sports bra to that list.

Whether you genuinely want to find the fastest woman in the world, believe women should have equitable health and access to our shared spaces, or simply want women to find as much joy in running as everyone deserves, it is essential for all of us to move forward with open eyes and ears on how our sport should change for the better for everybody.

OPPOSITE

Elite female athletes racing the streets of New York.

Sarah Ackland

Architect and activist

Underpinned by her doctoral research in the field of architecture, Sarah Ackland facilitates conversations around how women run through their built surroundings via her organization Taking Space.

HOW HAS YOUR RELATIONSHIP WITH THE URBAN ENVIRONMENT CHANGED THROUGH RUNNING?

Running makes you come up against the city harder. You spend more time outside actually hitting up against the city physically with your body, but then you form a closer, stronger connection to that city, and closer bonds with the people in it. How people can then not consider what that body they are in means, I find impossible.

WHAT DIFFICULTIES DO YOU FACE WHEN PLANNING YOUR RUNS?

For a lot of us, the way that we navigate our days, there's a lot of unconscious decision-making going on, which is exhausting. What route are you going to take? Where are you going to go? What are you going to wear? This is all something that anyone with an intersection is going to have to confront.

HOW CAN SOMEONE BEST UNDERSTAND WHY RUNNING IN CITIES CAN BE A STRUGGLE FOR WOMEN?

I always say to people, 'Put your body in a space and feel how much space you can take up.' I think if you actually take that reflective moment – to actually feel aware of how comfortable you are – I think you can unpick how others might feel in that space.

Taking
Space

Jessica Zapotechne

Girls Run NYC

Now a community builder with Adidas Runners, Jessie Zapo was an important early member of Bridgerunners, before eventually splintering off to create Girls Run NYC, an authentic space for women that has proven popular for over a decade.

WHY DID YOU START WOMEN-ONLY RUNNING SPACES?

I was getting to this point where I was training women for races. I had run a couple of marathons with not great training – just being ignorant and going for it. I realized there's more that you can do to make this a better experience and I wanted these other girls who would never run a marathon to do that. There were things that needed to happen, like track workouts, tempo runs and long runs. I was learning the pieces of training, and I was doing that within Bridgerunners, and even had this idea of creating this subgroup called Lady Bridgerunners. Saes said, 'I think maybe it's time to create your own thing.'

WHAT PROBLEMS STILL EXIST?

Sadly, violence against women is as high as it's ever been and it's still not safe to run by yourself. Then there's the argument that we're always going to need these spaces [like Girls Run] because it doesn't seem like that issue is going away. Women captains from Adidas Runners global community came together to work towards finding solutions to ending gender-based violence and we think it's not just a women's issue; it's a human issue.

WHAT ARE THE SOLUTIONS?

It starts with talking about it, and cultivating allyship. In order for real change to happen, we must have non-women allies in this fight. I think there is a lot of work that can be done that can help. I don't think gender-specific spaces are the answer, but they're a piece. The next piece is allyship, because there have to be co-ed spaces.

THE ALLURE OF FAME

There's something unique about being able to run the same course as both the marathon world record holder and the most famous member of One Direction, but that's what runners can do.

If you run the London Marathon today, you could be running with Mo Farah and Gordon Ramsay. Back in 1983, you could've been running with punk rock legend Joe Strummer, singer of The Clash, who prepared for the race by drinking ten pints of beer. Or, if you've run the Honolulu Marathon any time since the early 1980s you may have caught a glimpse of Haruki Murakami who has made it a near-on annual tradition to complete the race. What other sport can you so easily arrange to do that? A kickaround on the beach with Lionel Messi? A casual game of hoops with LeBron James? Racing Ronnie O'Sullivan to 147? Nope, but sign up to get your final World Marathon Major in Tokyo, and you might find yourself running alongside Harry Styles.

There's a very specific thrill to knowing that public figures *also* run, but why wouldn't they? It reminds me of moments in my former life as a music journalist when I discovered that multiple United States national soccer team goalkeepers listened to heavy metal. It was the juxtaposition of an athlete who plays a family-oriented sport listening to the same abrasive bands as my community.

Runners watching any movie in the *Mission Impossible* franchise will wonder, 'Why does Tom Cruise run like that?' Also, much chatter occurred when Taylor Swift rehearsed for the multibillion-dollar-grossing *Eras* tour by singing her sets while running on a treadmill, but it made perfect sense for the singer to practise for running across a 250ft (75m) stage while performing her songs. Similarly, Ben Gibbard plays to 20,000 people at the Hollywood Bowl when he's not running ultramarathons, and it's a combination that causes raised

OPPOSITE

Author Haruki Murakami.

Gillette
0918
LON

OPPOSITE AND ABOVE

Joe Strummer of The Clash at the 1983 London Marathon.

eyebrows with runners and rockers alike. It's unclear whether it's Death Cab for Cutie fans or people in the ultrarunning community who appreciate Gibbard's membership of their club more, but is there anything more incongruous than a star musician who can also run superhuman distances?

That gap between nightlife personalities and wellness campaigners is shrinking of late. Celebrities have been expanding the reach of the running world by organizing highly priced races. On the surface, it may feel like just another craven cash-in after one of their marketing team highlighted the rise of run clubs or a record-breaking number of marathons, but when these celebrities leverage the parasocial relationships to improve the health of their fans, they can effect real change. While female celebrities like Reese Witherspoon, Oprah and Dua Lipa start book clubs, thus choosing reading as their radical agent of transformation, the likes of DJ Diplo and Blink 182 drummer Travis Barker host and participate in simple pre-show run clubs, and comedian Bert Kreischer and rapper Jelly Roll invite their fans to track and celebrate their weight-loss progress as they embark upon a healthier lifestyle, using running.

Maybe the effect on public health is greater the more high profile a figure is. Take the President of the United States, for instance – arguably the most famous person in the world. A number of American presidents have been keen runners, with the Clinton–Gore administration even installing a 4ft-wide quarter-mile (1.2m×400m) track on the South Lawn of the White House back in 1993 because the road closures that resulted from President Clinton's public jogging habit proved too disruptive and expensive to DC traffic. When even the South Lawn proved too open an area for the President to exercise in safely, they installed a gym inside the White House, thus relieving his secret service detail of their mandatory daily miles. That meant that George W Bush jogged on the spongy track more frequently than his predecessor. His father, George HW Bush, also ran while in office, often with journalists. It was seen as an hour of solace from the rigours of the highest-pressure job in the world.

The 39th President, Jimmy Carter, picked up a daily running habit during the running boom of the 1970s, even inviting the winners of the 1979 Boston Marathon for dinner, no doubt bending their ears about training methods throughout. One running-related decision that he regretted until the day that he died, aged 100, was removing the USA from the 1980 Olympics in Moscow in response to the Soviet invasion of Afghanistan. It was the high point of American athletics after the running boom began, and the USA's absence at the Games ended careers. When the Soviet Union boycotted the 1984 Olympics in Los Angeles in retaliation, it put the results of those games under a cloud as well. Those geopolitics meant that it took a long time for American distance running to reach those heights again.

Running today is less about elite athletes than ever, so a call to arms by a millionaire celeb has more effect on getting everyday people up and running than maybe anything else out there. Running is the great equalizer, after all. No matter how many private chefs or luxury at-home gyms we have, once we're out there on the course, we've got nobody else to rely on but ourselves.

THE NEW STORYTELLING

What do you think about when you think about a runner? The idea of what a runner is, or who can be a runner, has changed drastically, and one of the reasons for that is the democratization of how we tell stories. It's human nature to want to tell our stories. It's how we connect with people and build community, and in this era of unprecedented communication, technology has been crucial in multiplying the number of ways that we can tell those stories, whether it's the run that we had today or the broader tale of what running has given our lives.

The doom-and-gloom message about the media is that books aren't selling, and magazines and newspapers are going under left, right and centre. Despite that narrative, people still want to consume stories. The Pew Research Center reports that Americans spend around 100 minutes a day getting their news, which is almost the same amount of time they spent in 2000. So what's actually changed? While we might have read the daily newspaper in the morning, or maybe just the big Sunday paper once a week, we now have a constant feed of new, bite-sized nuggets via our mobile phones. We used to watch 15 minutes of the breakfast news with our cereal, or listen to a few radio segments on the way to and from work, but now we likely get many of those clips online, and in a variety of methods, and we love that ease of information.

One story told in multiple ways is the Barkley Marathons. While it's always micro-blogged in real time by Keith Dunn, with the film *The Race That Eats Its Young* streaming on Netflix, there is also high-quality long-form storytelling available, and when Jasmin Paris completed the course in 2024, the only thing that story needed to reverberate around the world was David Miller's finish-line photograph (see page 52–53). Instagram is a place where photographers flourish. It's a place where they can instantly showcase their hard work capturing those era-defining frames filled with the intimacy of the moments that mean the most.

Another of my favourite examples of how one story has been told in multiple distinct ways is that of the Tarahumara. The indigenous tribe of Rarámuri, or 'running people', live a simple life farming in the Mexican Copper Canyons, near Chihuahua, and are notable for their elite endurance running while living on basic diets of corn and chia, and wearing simple leather *huaraches* with a discarded car tyre as the sole, rather than $170 trail shoes with high-tech midsoles. The fascinating story of this hidden-away civilization of runners was immortalized in one of the best-known running books of all time, *Born to Run* by Christopher McDougall, which unleashed a legion of barefoot runners as he pooh-poohed modern running-shoe technology at some riveting length.

The women of the Rarámuri are described by McDougall in glorious technicolour as wearing brightly coloured blouses and skirts as they ran free through the steep canyons they call home. The descriptions were apt and plentiful, but despite selling millions of copies of *Born to Run*, and no matter how brilliantly McDougall crafts the message of the Rarámuri, the story simply cannot reach everyone, because, for a whole variety of reasons, not everyone gets their information from books.

When a group of six Rarámuri women came to Los Angeles to take part in The Speed Project in spring 2024, The Ra Ra Ra team's story of racing hundreds of others across 340 miles (550km) of stark terrain, but in those multicoloured dresses and sandals rather than moisture-wicking technical apparel, was told effortlessly via Instagram to TSP's tens of thousands of followers around the world. Of course, the caption barely scratched the surface of what the tribe is, in comparison to what McDougall did, but that immediate, visual juxtaposition of their cerise, gold and green against the standard Speed Project runner clad in tonal polyester was catnip for that significant group of people who still want to be served up intriguing stories, but for whom maybe sitting down to read 50,000 words is too daunting. If a picture can tell a thousand words, that's enough for most.

One member of Rarámuri, Lorena Ramirez, is the subject of two different stories. The first was an eminently watchable 28-minute documentary called

OPPOSITE AND ABOVE

The RA RA RA team of Rarámuri women traverse the desert between LA and Las Vegas.

THERE AR
NO LIMITS
KINDS OF
WE CAN T

NOW
TO THE
STORIES
LL

Lorena, Light-Footed Woman that came out a decade after *Born to Run*. Then in 2024, a children's book, *Daughter of the Light-Footed People*, was released. Also based around Lorena's story as a champion marathoner, it's a wonderful way of delivering the tale of a magnificent woman and her magnificent culture to the next generation. It's a great way of normalizing long-distance races to pre-teens, anyway.

Through those four ways - two books, a Netflix documentary and Instagram - if you're meant to know about the Rarámuri, you will.

People want stories. We have a wealth of ways to find them. It's not that magazines and newspapers don't exist any more, or that books aren't being created. Multimillion-selling author Haruki Murakami, for instance, might be most well-known for *Norwegian Wood* or *Kafka on the Shore*, but among runners it's his 2007 ode to running, *What I Talk About When I Talk About Running* that comes to mind. As memoirs go, it's a hyper-specific love story that has turned countless readers into runners. Similarly, *Like the Wind* magazine first went to print in London in 2014 and has gone from strength to strength with its beautiful, high-quality, quarterly issues that are filled with dozens of long-form stories augmented perfectly by illustrations and photography. It feels like a luxurious treat to hold a copy in your hands every three months, but it's a completely different premise to the how-to guides of *Runner's World*, for instance. Yes, even within the magazine space that I trained in, there is much variety, and our world is all the richer for it.

Away from these more traditional avenues of storytelling, though, so many parts of the internet have democratized both who can tell their stories, and who gets to hear them. Even when a multinational burrito corporation engages with Strava, a platform where we each curate bite-sized stories detailing our running life, there is a wider narrative arc. When Chipotle set a challenge for the month of January 2025, where they offered a year's worth of free burritos to whoever ran one very specific 360m (400yd) loop in Tempe, Arizona, the most times, local ultrarunners Jamil Coury and Kevin Russ rose to the

OPPOSITE AND OVERLEAF

Jamil Coury and Kevin Russ during the Chipotle Challenge.

HAPPY BIRTHDAY
Normalize
High Mileage

HAPPY BIRTHDAY
SESSED

challenge. Both ran over 700 miles (1,130km) over the month, with Jamil running multiple 50-mile (80-km) days, and the details of the duo running the two city blocks were pored over on Reddit. The public went about their business completely oblivious to the mammoth double story of individual endurance unfolding around them.

Coury in particular – the owner of *Ultra Running Magazine* – filmed a plethora of content for his personal channels and even appeared on podcasts while trying to become the Local Legend (of both that Strava segment and his local Chipotle), thus capturing the attention of a huge audience. Strava shared a reel, filmmakers and luminaries of the trail running scene turned up for cameos, and Coury went through his car getting towed and an injury, losing the lead to Russ both times. It was that to-ing and fro-ing of the competition that got people riveted to their screens from thousands of miles away.

A fun metric calculated by Matt Trappe – a Boulder-based photographer who is deeply embedded within the trail community – is that Coury 'gathered an audience size similar to that of [Hoka], an account with 24x the follower base.' A hugely impressive feat, and one done by telling an amazing story. It was the kind of story where it didn't even matter who won. It was the most oddly scintillating event to follow along with, and somehow it made perfect sense. The new media has allowed more fringe stories to be told, which has led to more people seeing themselves as runners. Whether that's slow runners at the back of the pack like Martinus Evans, 'Runs With Emily' Shane, or Celina Stephenson explaining how one's pace is inconsequential, or former convicts documenting their path to multiple marathons in *Skid Row Marathon*, the brilliant 2017 documentary about Skid Row Running Club, or Louise Butcher who ran a marathon six weeks after a double mastectomy, and now continues to run marathons topless, you can't be what you can't see.

Running can give you an unparalleled period of reflection, where you can understand the limits of your body in real time. You go on wild excursions with your body and your mind. You consider where you're going, and what you need to get there – both literally and figuratively. As you begin to recognize patterns and collect experiences centred around your identity, it's natural to want to share your journey to self-discovery. You want to share how you've broken your body, and how you've healed it. You want to explain what you've learned about yourself, and how the world that you move through has treated you.

While marketing materials from the big brands mostly ignore the fringes of society, often preferring to focus on the wafer-thin white population, in the age of independent influencers a bold new format of left-field storytelling has emerged. People who understand where they have fitted into the running ecosystem tell personal stories that resonate deeply with everyday runners, often inspiring those readers, listeners and viewers to take their first steps. Consider how Instagram accounts for niche run clubs like Asian Trail Mix or Queer Run Club can be found freely, allowing people to find community so much more easily than in the past.

By exposing bold, previously unspoken new narratives, we have revolutionized uptake of runners in the grassroots of the sport. There are now no limits to the kinds of stories we can tell, and it's increasingly the case that anybody is able to tell them. As the running world has grown to include a more diverse picture of runners, the narratives are spinning a richer and richer tapestry every day, showing that anyone can be a runner.

Nils Arend

The Speed Project

When a group of friends decided to run from the Santa Monica Pier in Los Angeles to the Welcome to Las Vegas sign back in 2013, they weren't sure it was going to be any more than that one trip, but the images that came back from documenting a bunch of friends on a two-day journey across the stark terrain together ensured the event's immortality. Now, teams travel from around the world to compete in the race.

WHY DO YOU THINK THE SPEED PROJECT IS SO POPULAR?
People were amazed by the opportunity to experience something out of the norm. I didn't even know how the running world saw it because I wasn't part of it.

HOW HAS THE RUNNING WORLD CHANGED SINCE THE FIRST TSP?
The interesting thing with running is that 10 years ago running was a sport, and now running has become a lifestyle. It's enriched by other elements: music; fashion; certain event formats. So when you say 'running culture', I think about running as a lifestyle, not just a sport.

HOW DID YOU HARNESS THE POWER OF THE INTERNET?
When Instagram became a thing, it connected me with like-minded runners around the world. That's when I met Mike Saes, the NBRO folks and Charlie Dark, and I was like, 'Hey, I just ran from LA to Vegas with my friends and we made an 18-minute film. Do you want to show it to your community?' There was no unconventional content in running at the time. It just didn't exist, and

everybody was excited about it and especially this early stage of urban running culture, and then we did screenings around the world in 25 different cities. When I say screenings, I mean people huddling around a computer.

HOW NORMAL IS IT TO CREATE A RUNNING DOCUMENTARY NOW?
I had this funny idea that we're gonna give anybody who creates a film about their Speed Project experience a T-shirt: 'I also made a TSP documentary'. But everyone thought it was too passive-aggressive, so we didn't do it.

WHAT DO YOU BRING TO TSP?
It's influenced by my punk rock backbone and attitude, but it's not just demolition for the sake of destroying something. We're breaking something with a clear intention to get to a specific result. I think a lot of people are drawn to The Speed Project because there's a thread. There's a meaning behind it.

WHY CREATE AN EVEN MORE EXTREME EDITION IN ATACAMA?
One of the main things is that I need to stay motivated, and I need to be excited. Even a few months before TSP Atacama, I was very close to pulling the plug on LA to Vegas. It was getting too hyped and I felt like it wasn't representing me. I'm all about radical decisions if they're for the right reasons.

Usually everybody is on a high at the [closing] pool party, and I often get approached to bring The Speed Project to blank. The same thing happened in 2022. I was approached by MAFFs, an amazing group of Chilean runners.

My previous relationship to Chile started when we hosted a photo contest within the framework of our decentralized race during the pandemic. The winning photographer was a Chilean photographer, and his images felt otherworldly and really amazing, so when I met the MAFFs, who were the ones he photographed, we had this immediate amazing family vibe. I like vibrations and love, and it was just there.

SUNSEEKER
BY FOREST RIVER
EL MONTE RV
9FAY059
M-246196

OPPOSITE AND ABOVE

Missives from The Speed Project.

Simon Freeman

Publisher of **Like the Wind** magazine

Launching a new high-quality, boutique running magazine in 2014, just as the internet was collectively pivoting to video, putting journalists out of work left, right and centre, was a bold move. Now, over a decade in, having published hundreds of stories told by world-class writers, illustrators and athletes, the husband-and-wife team behind *Like the Wind* magazine is thriving like never before.

WHY DID YOU START A PRINT MAGAZINE?

The reason Julie (Freeman, co-founder) and I started a magazine is because this is the best medium for the types of stories we wanted to tell. Maybe a book, but some sort of printed matter. Something where you could take a minute over. I really loved magazines. I was buying *The Surfer's Journal* and *Rouleur* despite not owning a surfboard or a bicycle. I just liked the style and format.

WHY DO YOU THINK A PRINT MAGAZINE HAS SURVIVED IN THE DIGITAL AGE?

When we launched the magazine over 10 years ago, there was the consensus that everything was going online, and social media was taking over, but it was already very fast, short-format content. I think the world takeover by social media has continued at a pace, almost to the point that people are starting to push back.

I fully expect people to be on social media, listen to podcasts, watch videos, but also have a magazine so that twice a week for 20 minutes, they sit down with a cup of coffee and read a story. To me it's an 'and'.

WHAT IS THE VALUE OF DEEP STORYTELLING IN RUNNING?

Running is such a fundamental human activity that developed from the basic act of locomotion. There is very little complexity – the task is almost always getting from point A to point B as fast as possible. In that sense, running is a blank canvas on which it's natural that people want to paint their own stories.

If you listen to commentary about the sport of running, versus other sports, there usually isn't as much to say about the action itself. The stories behind the action are what brings the running to life. I also believe that running is an activity in which almost everyone can and does – more or less regularly – participate (or at least most people have run at some point in their lives). So our interest is less in 'how' someone runs – we all know how to run – but more 'why' people run.

WHY DO SO MANY STORIES COME OUT OF THE WORLD RUNNING?

While running is essentially the same activity of putting one foot in front of another, over and over, you only need to see a child running in the playground, a sprinter flying down the track at the Olympics, a mother completing a 100 mile ultra marathon crossing the finish line holding her children's hands and a couch-to-5K runner completing their first non-stop run, to understand that running has infinite versions. And that is before you get into what is going on in the heads of all the people running.

This huge variety of experiences – physical and emotional – means there are endless stories. I enjoy speaking to two or three people who have just finished the same run and asking them about their experiences. It is astounding how different their reports will be.

WHY DO RUNNERS RESPOND TO THESE STORIES?

I believe one of the most important reasons is that runners crave peeking into other people's experiences. I know what I feel, what I have seen and the experiences I have had as a runner. Naturally, the voyeur in me is endlessly curious about what other people have discovered about themselves, or the world, through running.

TOUCHING GRASS

Every action demands a reaction, and we now spend 40 per cent of our waking hours looking at a screen – an 8 per cent increase from 2012 to 2025. It's not natural. Human beings have evolved over millennia to be physical beasts who move for a living. The increasing industrialization and digitization of our lives have led to this series of running booms, which are, ultimately, moments of crisis, where we have collectively reacted to a new imbalance in our nature.

In an age where many Millennials and younger generations self-identify as being 'terminally online', when someone tells you that you've been on the internet for a little too long today, it's normal to suggest that we touch grass. Taken literally, the act of rolling around on a lawn is genuinely quite pleasant, but if we understand that spending a huge amount of our time on our laptops and phones requires some balance, and we've already identified the need for running as a perfect counterweight to our eight hours of sitting down, then what could be more diametrically opposed to looking at a screen while sitting in an artificially lit, climate-controlled room than running through nature?

We can't be completely tech-free on the trails, of course. GPS and emergency communication methods are important for safety, but those are the only real essentials. Beyond that you can luxuriate in spending an inordinate amount of time away from all other responsibilities and distractions, with every facet of trail running leaning towards the extremes of what you can find in other areas of running.

OPPOSITE

Trail runners race in Colorado, USA.

OVERLEAF

Mathieu Blanchard competes in the UTMB.

PAT'S RUN
3296
4664
PIKES PEAK ROAD RUNNERS
2969
4062
4356

RACE

ciele
mon

Getting out onto the trails is seen by many as the final boss level of running. Running through wilderness is more natural than running through the built environment, so it's seen as an escape from the drudgery of everyday life, and the meteoric growth of the sport is evidence of that. The numbers bandied around outline the increase in ultramarathons in the USA from 233 in 2000 to 2,033 in 2023, as well as a 2,394 per cent growth in trail running participation between 2001 and 2022 according to the most thorough report out there, by shoe comparison website RunRepeat. To keep trail running in the correct perspective, though, current estimates also suggest there are over three times as many road runners as trail runners.

That disparity between the numbers of road and trail runners should be no surprise considering the unique understanding of both body and mind you need to endure the distances and terrains in trail and ultra. Just as you can achieve the runner's high after a few miles of running local streets, it goes a little further when you're running 100 miles (161km). Hallucinations abound, but no recreational drugs have been required. Any money you save on illicit substances, however, has to be re-budgeted for the flasks, flashlights, food, first-aid kit and warm-, cold- and wet-weather gear you have to carry with you on these expeditions – stuff that you don't need when you're running around your town. It's tantamount to camping culture, and it really doesn't come cheap.

The payoff is extended time in nature, and running outdoors really leads to a love story. How can you not become the staunchest advocate for the parks that you spend so much time traversing, and the people within them? When you're 30 hours into an ultramarathon, and a stranger is cooking you a meal at an aid station, that intimacy is amplified one hundredfold. It's difficult to recreate the community that is built on the trails. Then, between those aid stations, you're alone with your thoughts for hours upon end, getting into scrapes and understanding how the land needs you as much as you need it. It's impossible to leave such adventures without a story of your own. Whether it's one of the many magnificent women like Sophie Power or 'Lactating' Laura Vaughan, who performed a similar feat to Sophie in 1996, when she ran the Wasatch 100, breastfeeding her son at aid stations, or someone like Dean Karnazes or Russ Cook (AKA Hardest Geezer), who made their names crossing entire continents, every story is bigger and more extreme.

ABOVE

Kílian Jornet competes in the Western States Endurance Race.

While the demographic disparities are also more pronounced with increasingly extreme distances, young women are a driving force behind the boom in sub-ultra-distance runs, with some races even achieving gender parity. It'll take time until racial minorities are fully represented on the trails, but the desire is there, and the work is being done in a young sport.

Indeed, trail running on the whole is incredibly fresh-faced – one of the last vestiges of uncommercialized sports. Sponsors are still more likely to be trail-related brands, rather than international banking powerhouses. Right now, long-time trail enthusiasts know one another in a small but growing community, and it's a cosy club. But for how long? The community reminds me a lot of Twitter when it first launched in 2006. It was filled with tech nerds and journalists who were eager to find out the potential of this new communication tool, so the energy was so positive, and newcomers were welcomed. Back then only 10 per cent of the world had the internet constantly at their fingertips, versus 90 per cent now. As more and more people figure out the beauty of trail running, the goal is to maintain its purity as much as possible. It will be down to the stewards of the sport to take their responsibility seriously as increasingly high-stakes opportunities, and audiences, come their way.

CHINA'S BIG OPPORTUNITY

It's easy to focus on the USA and the Alpine countries for trail running, but there might be more opportunities further afield. Several countries with gloriously varied terrain (ancient volcanoes, tropical forests and long, scenic coastlines) and suitably strong histories in the outdoors, such as Nepal and New Zealand, as well as several countries in Latin America, all have huge potential to add to the rich culture in trail running. But it's China, with its population of 1.4 billion, that many expect to surpass the United States as the largest trail running community in the world.

Organized trail running is a new sport in China, only going back to the 2013 Ninghai 100-miler, which takes place in East China's mountains, following part of the country's first 300-mile (500-km) hiking trail. This happened very deliberately. Because the enormous country boasts a wide spectrum of technical landscapes, including desert and forest as well as mountain and dirt trail, sports tourism was highlighted as an avenue for the country's economic growth in the 12th Five-Year Plan for Economic and Social Development of the People's Republic of China that took place between 2011 and 2015. With local governments encouraged to grow the sport by putting on outdoor events in order to become one of hundreds, and maybe thousands, of 'sports and leisure specialty towns', China fast became a trail runner's dream.

Indeed, by the end of 2019, China's race calendar had grown to include around 500 races, with 50 per cent of Yunnan Province's GDP coming from tourism. However, it didn't really recover after the double hit of the pandemic's strict lockdowns and then the tragedy of the Gansu ultramarathon in 2021, where 21 of the 172 runners died from hyperthermia after an unexpected change in weather. The Chinese government investigated ultramarathons for a year afterwards, so there were just 90 races on the books in 2022, but that has resulted in top-class safety regulations. Ultra-Trail du Mont Blanc's 2023 announcement that their World Series would include Chinese races going forward was a welcome one. A global entity like UTMB coming in and really kick-starting the trail world showed that China had landed firmly on the global trail running map. Cut to 2025 and there are five different UTMB races in China, including Ninghai, of course.

The beautiful thing about a country as large as China is how they can create, draw on and encourage their own culture with such precision and ease. The phenomenon of *guochao* is a popular organic trend with the quarter-billion-strong Gen Z cohort, where increased feelings of national pride and cultural curiosity has led to the younger generation plumping for domestic brands like Nedao and Kailas over foreign imports such as Nike or Adidas. Trail running has attracted young Chinese people from traditional running, but also from outdoor sports like skiing and hiking, and they love flaunting their lifestyles on native social media like RedNote, Douyin and WeChat as much as their Western compatriots do on theirs, and pushing the stylish *guochao* narrative online. They even have their own version of Strava, called Gudong.

That personal desire to engage with Chinese heritage in the landscape fits neatly into the idea of *guochao*, so when, along with the race announcements, UTMB also partnered with Chinese brand Aonijie, it made perfect business sense all round. You can point to a 40-year erosion of communism, with unfettered capitalism taking its place, or the related burgeoning middle class that is more financially able to participate in trail running, but the people soon found the same benefits to running beyond physical, mechanical health that everyone else has.

Interestingly, China's 14th Five-Year Plan took place between 2021 and 2025, and was focused on developing national sports infrastructure and promoting outdoor sports, with a goal of transforming China into a global sporting powerhouse by 2035 by aiming both to get the whole population more active, but also in terms of producing more elite professional athletes. As trail running continues its inexorable rise, everything affiliated with it will remain a large part of that development. Aonijie, for instance, doesn't yet sit on the shelves with Salomon and Arc'teryx in the USA or Europe but, with 45 per cent of those two brands being owned by Chinese mega-brand Alta, export could be a goal, or sales in China could suffice. They have the growing audience for it, after all.

There are many parallels to be drawn there with Chinese athletes. The data from UTMB Chamonix shows that there was an increasing number of Chinese finishers at the prestigious race up until 2019, where they were the fifth-largest foreign contingent, but the same problems that plagued the domestic scene following the pandemic appear to have affected the top athletes, and participation fell away. If both the Chinese government and the biggest international brands in trail are putting their money on the Chinese trail running scene, however, increasing numbers of Chinese athletes finishing races abroad, maybe even wearing a Chinese brand on the podium, is certainly on the horizon. As always, the view from the top will be worth it.

OPPOSITE

Runners compete in the Ultra-Trail Ninghai, China.

可隆东海云顶跑山赛
KOLON SPORT TRAIL RACE 2025

Dylan Bowman

Professional trail running athlete

In 2013, he was the youngest runner in the top ten of the Western States Endurance Run when he finished fifth, and he went on to reach podiums all around the world. Now Bowman runs the Freetrail network, a media organization 'dedicated to changing people's lives through the great sport of trail running'.

WHAT HAS CHANGED IN THE WORLD OF ULTRAMARATHONS?
Literally everything. We've been on this rocket-ship growth trajectory, and it's felt like it's been exponential the entire time. The biggest thing that's changed is that it went from being this grassroots subculture into a mature industry or sport. There's still a lot of room to grow, but it emerged from the backwoods of obscurity.

ARE THERE ANY DOWNSIDES TO THAT LEVEL OF GROWTH?
Naturally, it means that even though the market is growing, it means more and more people are making a living within the sport, which is a good thing, but it also means there is more misaligned incentives and more competition, which in some way diminishes the feel that this is a tight-knit grassroots community.

When I started Freetrail, I had these rose-coloured glasses that trail running was different, and as we grew our culture would rise above all challenges and keep us all connected during any periods of disagreement. With the sport maturing, naturally the market dynamics are felt in the core of the community. How do mom-and-pop race directors continue to exist alongside the juggernauts of the sport?

WHAT'S STILL MISSING FROM TRAIL RUNNING?

I think it's a very confusing sport if you're not deep within it. There are so many different race series, and you don't really know which one does what. It's not easy to understand how you get into the Western States lottery or accumulate UTMB stones or what's the difference between UTMB and the Golden Trail Race Series. Any person can throw on an NBA game and understand what the dynamics are from a league level and who the good players are, but it's kinda hard to be a fan of trail without spending an insane amount of time understanding all of these nuances. We may be at that apex of fragmentation now where things will start coming together in a way that feels a little more cogent to the casual observer.

Catherine Poletti

Co-Founder and Chairwoman
of Ultra-Trail du Mont Blanc

Alongside her husband Michael, Catherine Poletti has created the most competitive and influential ultrarunning event on the trail running calendar. Over 20 years after the UTMB's inception, the Polettis are still active stewards as the sport races exponentially towards mainstream acknowledgement.

WHAT HAS BEEN THE BIGGEST CHANGE IN TRAIL RUNNING OVER THE PAST TWO DECADES?

Twenty years ago, trail running wasn't so popular. It was understood as a sport for the people who are a little bit older, because it was a way of life more than a sport. We saw the change appear in 2008. In the event Kílian Jornet won and he was only 20 years old. I think this is the moment where everything changed because immediately the sport seemed more fun, with the possibility to work on the performance. It was the moment where we started to have more and more elite road runners, and it became more of a sport.

WHY DO YOU THINK TRAIL RUNNING HAS GAINED SO MUCH POPULARITY?

Running a marathon is a way to visit a town – to mix running and a sort of tourism. We have the same thing in trail running, but instead of a town, you visit the land, the mountain. I think this double interest is the reason why.

AS THE SPORT GROWS, WHAT IS THE BEST WAY TO MAINTAIN THE INTEGRITY OF TRAIL RUNNING?

First are the values and the vision. We need to keep an authentic activity. That means to respect the place where you are, the inhabitants, and the environment – not to make something that is like Disney World. You have to respect the people you are with, respect the nature you are running through, to respect yourself, the other runners, and the volunteers. Respect is one of the main values we have to deploy on all sides.

UTMB HAS EXPANDED DEEPLY INTO CHINA

We had some franchises there in 2014 but those two races stopped because of Covid and the very, very big accident in the Yellow Mountains where 21 people who died. We began again [in 2022] and now we have five different events in China, and probably two more in 2026.

It doesn't depend only on us. Each time we have a franchise, we work with a local organizer to provide local runners with a UTMB experience near where they live. China is between a country and a continent. You don't have the same thing in the region of Beijing and Szechuan. It depends on the capacity to meet a good team. We need to find people with the same values as us. It's really important that they trust us and we trust them.

HOW MUCH FARTHER CAN UTMB GROW?

I think we can do even more in the UTMB World Series. We created an endowment fund. A foundation to be able to support some big associations about the environment. We work a lot with this foundation and will continue to develop it, because I think it's the way to keep the values [of UTMB], and keep it as something that is not only a business.

We are not against the money. The money can be a good thing depending on how you spend it. It's not a problem. I'm happy to have a very successful business because it's allowed us to spend the money to do something really interesting and – we think – important.

12

2

TESTING THE LIMITS

If the meaning of life is exploration, then finding our limits as humans is the most natural thing we can do, and searching for our maximums is the root of evolution and of our storied histories. From ancient humans gaining arched feet and lengthening their Achilles tendons via persistent hunting of large game over long distances, through the death of legendary Greek messenger Pheidippides (whose feats would go on to inspire some to pursue the fabled sub-two-hour marathon), running has always been the gold standard of finding – and pushing – the human limit.

Both of these necessary reasons for everyday running have dissipated over time as we developed weaponry and farming so that we could move past running to hunt to feed your family, and found that horses, cars or the internet were more efficient for delivering messages. However, running for sporting spectacle and pedigree, however, will never be defeated. As such, records and milestones are constantly being broken by everyone from schoolkids and elite marathoners through Boston hopefuls and 300-mile ultra-trail runners. Competitive running has been distilled to its purest purpose, so is now the time that the rest of us can shake off the shackles of constant improvement with a view to running for pleasure? Comparison, after all, is the thief of joy.

There are several significant obstacles standing in the way of the amateur enthusiast's goal of running for happiness. With the deluge of information that the digital revolution has foisted upon us, we have to actively avoid the measuring and comparison made possible by the slew of running metrics our watches and trackers immediately send to our smartphones. There are oodles of readily accessible research into the optimal number of grams of carbohydrates to chug down during a long run to both prevent bonking (AKA hitting The Wall – the sudden onset of fatigue that many runners suffer in later stages of the marathon due to depleted energy stores) and optimize (that word) recovery. This information can be augmented with our own fastidious logging of our meals on our app of choice. The result is that we know what macros our bodies need, and when. Hence, the energy gels that were first formulated in the 1990s are now commonplace, and we're in a world of supplements for everything from protein and electrolytes to creatine and magnesium. All with the goal of optimizing (that word again) our lives.

It's that concept of the quantified self. We're spending an inordinate amount of time poring over the data with a view to hacking our lives. The goal is accuracy, but it's also control, in a time when each new generation feels like they have less control than their predecessors. With diminishing job security coupled with the vagaries of online dating leaving all unsatisfied, more of Gen Z is choosing to spend their time training to run a marathon, with a third of 2026 London Marathon entries coming from the age group. In Los Angeles, 28 per cent of finishers at the 2024 LA Marathon were in their twenties, versus 21 per cent in 2019. Maggie Mertens, author of *Better Faster Farther*, wrote in *The Atlantic* in 2024 about the 'quarter-life crisis', where she posits that the behaviour stems from frustrations around poor opportunities in both their professional and love lives. In reality, that control is simply the manifestation of a search for self-actualization, and the data is enabling it in newfound ways.

The quantified self is a leading component of marginal-gains culture. The underlying theory behind cycling guru Dave Brailsford's concept of personal improvement was to improve by 1 per cent in multiple areas by using activity data, supplements and equipment to see larger compound improvements overall, so getting a new shoe, the Vaporfly, that promises up to 4 per cent increases in running efficiency was massive. That shoe truly made the sub-two-hour marathon seem possible, inspiring a generation of civilians to wonder what their own bodies could do.

OVERLEAF

Mathieu Blanchard at the finish line of the UTMB.

DACIA
wahoo
UTMB
SAVOIE
MONT-BLANC
HOKA
UTMB WORLD SERIES
UTMB
WORLD SERIES
UTMB
MONT-BLANC
HOKA
FLY HUMAN FLY

UTMB
HOKA
FLY HUMAN FLY
DACIA
wahoo
CHAMONIX
UTMB
MONT-BLANC
WORLD
SERIES

Currently, the official world record of 2:00:35 is held by the late Kelvin Kiptum, who died in a car accident just four months after his October 2023 victory in Chicago. He was just 24 years old. Kipchoge achieved his fastest marathon time when he was a decade older, so we can only wonder what Kiptum may have been capable of.

There has been some research into the human limits of marathoning, however. A 2019 statistical model built by Dr Simon Angus of Monash University in Melbourne, Australia, suggested that the arrival of world records follows a pattern, and predicted that there is a 1 in 10 chance that the two-hour mark will be reached by May 2032, with a headline prediction that 1:58:05 is the current human limit of how fast a marathon could be run. With Kiptum's outstanding effort, though, an updated model by Dr Angus brought that time forward by over five years to March 2027, taking the human limit down to 1:55:40. The model gives women just a 1 per cent chance of ever running a sub-two-hour marathon, estimating the fastest possible female marathon time at 2:05:31.

These are all predictions based on the current conditions and technologies available. Something that gives the prediction added credence is that Dr Angus, who is an endurance runner himself, takes into account the barriers and limitations that women face, and encourages both public and private sectors to work hard to increase opportunities for elite female athletic performance. He suggests that there are likely potential world record holders out there, particularly in Africa, that we might simply never know about, due to reduced accessibility to sport.

What your body can do when you can dedicate your whole life to training for a single race, with chefs and scientists dialling in your nutrition for you, coaches ensuring your training schedule is perfect, and psychologists setting your mindset to win is one thing. What you can do when you have to fit in making lunches for the kids before dropping them off at two different schools ahead of a 90-minute commute is quite another. Is the extra grind of taking ten minutes off your marathon compatible with the grind that you're already performing on a daily basis? Consider that you run for your leisure. Consider that running could be a source of fun. Consider that fun doesn't have to involve winning.

THE CAPITALIST MINDSET OF RUNNING

We live in a world fuelled by capitalism. It's not in the Constitution of the United States, but it was a question in my American citizenship exam. Capitalism is as American as apple pie, but it's also as American as the pursuit of happiness, which is in the Constitution. The capitalism part of the equation, however, means that happiness is an eternal pursuit, because nothing is ever enough in that eternal-growth mindset. We just have to get more money, better shareholder satisfaction, more everything. Forever.

We compete because records are there to be broken. Despite accepting the physical limit to how fast a human can run a marathon, still we try, because running has the same eternal capitalistic growth demands coursing through its veins. However, just as Kipchoge retired from Olympic marathoning after Paris in 2024, there is also an incredibly human time limit to this growth. Our bodies simply can't do more forever. We get old. We peak at 30 to 35 years of age before the inevitable decline sets in. Then what? You can measure your times against ever-increasing age brackets, but can you find true happiness when you know your personal record from this year isn't as fast as last year's? Is improvement and achievement really our only path to happiness? The answer might be in capitalism's opposite philosophy: sustainability.

Whether we're talking about sustainability in terms of the environment or within our own selves, the idea is brought into sharper focus with every news headline about disasters around the planet, and a growing mental health crisis. Perhaps making changes to achieve happiness on a personal level – affecting only those directly around us – may be the brightest path forward. It's progress, but maybe not as we've previously been sold it.

'Happiness is desirable, but it is a by-product, the result of a way of life, not a goal which is forever beyond one's grasp. To make happiness the goal is to kill it in advance.' So said Henry Miller, in *Stand Still Like the Hummingbird.*

If we run with sustainability as our primary focus, we might begin to think about how to keep doing this thing that we love – running – forever, but without the shackles of recorded times and distances; without the associated fear of failure constantly looming overhead. We might start running more gently so that we haven't torn apart every fibre in our legs by the time we're 40, so as to enjoy the side-effect of the runner's high instead. We can run in the

NN
KIPCHOGE

morning to use sunlight to power our circadian rhythms, and run to get those 45 minutes of cardiovascular exercise three times a week as the doctor has always suggested. It's the idea of an atelic activity, where you do something for the pure joy of doing it, without the requirement of a specific goal or outcome. You can focus on the process, and the craft.

Maybe that idea of ditching your smartwatch completely, removing all metrics, comes into play here. Part of this big idea is working to shift running away from being your entire identity. Figuring out what running does for you is a great first step to finding out an alternative activity when you're injured, for instance. I see injury and illness as an inevitability of life. A list that I've long paid attention to is the five key Buddhist remembrances, which say that we will have ill health, we will grow old, we will die, everything around us is subject to change, and our actions are the only thing that is true of us. Remembering that these things are certainties, and that it's all largely out of our control, is a great way of focusing on the most important things in life. It's the pathway to enlightenment, and a very Zen method of finding oneself.

My favorite modern philosopher had his own views on achieving that, and realizing one's potential. Some of the best advice that I've ever read to find the truest path on the journey of life came from Hunter S Thompson who was just 22 years old when he wrote a letter to his friend Hume Logan following a request for life advice. His central premise revolved around the decision of 'whether to float with the tide, or to swim for a goal.' Another thought around self-actualization, perhaps, but the wisdom was centered around understanding oneself first and foremost, rather than understanding a tangible goal – the more common occurrence – and be prepared for that understanding to change as you do as a person.

Thompson posits, 'Is it worth giving up what I have to look for something better?' Only you can make that choice, but you're certainly more likely to find happiness having put the thought into finding your truest meaning. It's a different kind of limit, but certainly one that's worth searching for.

OPPOSITE

Kipchoge wins the Tokyo Marathon in 2022.

3

THE FUTURE OF RUNNING

We've been enjoying a succession of running booms over the past quarter of a century and there are no signs of the growth slowing. There are certainly no signs of a bust. In fact, the future of running will almost certainly continue to be centred around those ego metrics of faster and further. Records will always be there to be broken, and we have the bodies and the desire to break them. As running as a subculture continues to grow and bleed further into the mainstream, however, I predict the growth will increasingly come from fringe and minority communities. The conversation around running will show more diverse thinking to match this.

How can we talk about the future without thinking about sustainability? That includes the sustainability of both our own running practices and that of the world through which we run. As runners, we spend more time outside than the average person, and with increasing numbers of climate-related disaster events occurring every year, that has to concern us. Just as running a marathon through city smog or wildfire smoke is not a tenable situation, writing a race calendar around an ever-expanding wildfire season is as absurd as it is increasingly unrealistic. So what's the solution in a world that can feel increasingly futureless? Do we cave in and take the dopamine-fuelled path of least resistance, or do we fight to build the world that will reward us long after we're gone?

What if the thousands of people flying to marathons around the world seven, eight or nine times in a year just to get *another* medal leads to enough excess consumption that the air quality somewhere far away becomes too poor for people there to run? Is the trinket worth it? We're much more willing to understand the severity of the situation when it comes to celebrities and their private jets – Taylor Swift got plenty of criticism during that *Eras* tour – but are you absolved from your resource-wasting behaviour just because you're engaging in something healthy?

The reality is that runners are adventurers. We love to explore, whether that's on a micro level during our daily runs or on the macro level as we jet around the world to take in foreign surroundings at pace. That's why the larger marathons are so difficult to gain a place at, and that trend isn't going away. But if the big races are constantly sold out, would they be able to host a second edition the following weekend (without the elite runners, perhaps) in order to accommodate more runners that just want to run that city? It's what Coachella Festival introduced in 2012. The same lineup of musicians in the same Californian desert location over two successive weekends, allowing more music lovers to experience the festival. The big question is whether the cities (London, New York, Paris) could handle the upheaval for another weekend, but the hundreds of millions of dollars a race boosts the economy of a host city might be the carrot required to change the local government's minds.

A lot of top-level messaging about environmental sustainability focuses on the individual, so maybe the onus should be on the people in charge. Get race insurance, for instance, so that if your race is cancelled because of an environmental calamity, at least you'll be covered. What if the race directors made race T-shirts an optional purchase, rather than creating thousands of units of wasted clothing, and you had to bring a reusable cup for drinking fluids on the course, cutting out thousands of disposable cups in landfill? Would we give up some of our marginal gains and souvenirs to ensure we have a planet to run on? Could we?

How about the people creating the goods? What if the brands did more to make the creation of their apparel less wasteful? What if the increase in fashion in running means that we can wear our running gear comfortably in our daily lives first, and then wear it to run in? Can we run in our clothes more than once before laundry day? It might involve choosing more natural fibres, but it's possible. Just as we cannot live in a vacuum, we cannot run in a vacuum. Every run is a political act connected to people and place all around the planet.

What will the next industrial revolution bring? Where will the next wave of software take us? The Fourth Industrial Revolution AKA Industry 4.0, because it is so overwhelmingly computer-driven in nature, is starting to be felt in the real world. All the cinematic ruminations had us believing that we'd be inhabiting a future filled with flying cars and advanced virtual reality, but it seems that the modern day's digital solutions have instead led to increased solitude. That yearning for real connection has meant that run clubs have become an important human balance to that.

Another option to increase human connection while running but incorporating technology is to run with a virtual partner. For those who live in areas too remote to sustain an in-person community, the idea of dialling into a chat with others on their long run running at the same pace could become a viable option. This connection could come from a dedicated forum that you are already a part of, or it could be a new feature of an existing app. You might already enjoy the companionship of the pre-recorded guided runs found on the Nike Run Club app, this is a complex but logical extension. A pie-in-the-sky idea, perhaps, but until the Luddites somehow win the battle against technology encroaching upon every part of our lives, it remains an option.

How about virtual and augmented reality? There are many avenues to use that technology in both training and apparel. We've already seen low-cost, low-quality artificial intelligence take over parts of the civilian coaching industry, but are they really any worse than the training plans you could already find online? With wearable tech improving with every new model, there is a strong case for our biometric and nutrition data to be incorporated with our daily movement schedules to improve both our training and recovery plans with every passing year.

Imagine a world where our biomechanics and running form can be analyzed using a video taken on the phones we already own for a nominal, automated fee rather than via a series of expensive sessions with a human expert. That new and constantly improving data can be used in the same way: to enhance performance by both optimizing running economy and reducing the risk of injury – meaning no lengthy absences from training. For those irrevocably wedded to the idea of biohacking their way to faster and faster race times, it's an inviting proposition.

For the other faction of runners ready to revolt against the never-ending metrics in favour of focusing on their mental health, the ever-deepening understanding of the field will be integrated into coaching philosophies so we will train using increasingly holistic methods.

What else can our machines do for us? Those 3-D shoes printed in bulk are certainly a headline event but, closer to the coaching side of things, there will be body scans by our personal devices that will measure us in situ, allowing us to run faster, for longer. Even though we're seeing production increase in real time, the logistics of getting a $300 shoe printed remotely are still difficult to fathom right now, but a set of custom insoles that arrive in your mailbox perfectly moulded to your foot? Yeah, we can probably already do that, and we can probably already accept that service into our lives.

The thing about running is that while it can be very easily augmented by technology, when you boil running down to its purest essence, it's just about a person - you - and your desire to run. The high-tech adornments are only for the wealthiest runners. Everyone else will run for as long as they have clean air to breathe. In this increasingly democratized world, you will have the choice to engage with the world exactly how you want. Running is a radical act, and neither the world nor you will ever stop changing.

Importantly, both running and reading are leisure pursuits, so the goal there is to find happiness and pleasure. We're taking the time to try and improve our lives just one iota. If you can read this book and find a single passage that reframes one thing in your reality, I will have succeeded in my quest to help you find more happiness, compassion and love for the past, present and future of this world that we share.

Further Watching

26.2 TO LIFE

(2022)

A documentary about the residents of San Quentin State Prison - California's most notorious maximum-security correctional facility. The story? Inmates train to run a marathon inside San Quentin by running 105 quarter-mile laps of the prison yard.

3100: RUN AND BECOME

(2018)

It would be beyond reason that anyone would run thousands of miles around a single block of NYC but for the storytelling in this film - a beautiful and uplifting detailing of the essential spiritual side of this race.

THE BARKLEY MARATHONS: THE RACE THAT EATS ITS YOUNG

(2014)

This film is a wild peek into one of the most fascinatingly secretive races in the ultra running world. If you want to understand how and why participants take themselves to their mental and physical limits, this is a must-watch.

BRITTANY RUNS A MARATHON

(2019)

The easiest watch on this list, this is a relatable story about a hard-partying woman in the city who turns to running to turn her unhealthy lifestyle around. This film has repeatedly been credited as the starting point for many a runner's journey.

PREFONTAINE & WITHOUT LIMITS

(1997) & (1998)

It often happens in Hollywood that two incredibly similar movies are released in close proximity, and that happened with these two sporting biopics about Steve Prefontaine. Opinion is split on which is better, so watch both and decide for yourself. I'm a Billy Crudup fan.

THE SOURCE

(2019)

A short film about arguably the greatest American ultra runner's attempt to complete the Tahoe 200-mile race in under 48 hours. It's another fascinating insight into how the best can conquer new frontiers while retaining their humanity.

SKID ROW MARATHON

(2017)

This film is about Craig Mitchell, a Los Angeles Superior Court Judge. He is also the founder of the Skid Row Running Club, a secular non-profit organization that has helped thousands overcome the effects of substance use disorder and homelessness using the power of running.

THE SPEED PROJECT

(2013)

There are thousands of ultra-polished mini-documentaries detailing the gruelling course(s) from Los Angeles to Las Vegas littering YouTube today. They're produced by everyone from local run clubs to multi-billion-dollar brands, but back in 2013 there was only one. The energy in the original is inimitable.

UNBREAKABLE – THE WESTERN STATES 100

(2012)

Yes, it's another 21st-century film about ultra running (there's something about superhuman feats that humans feel compelled to document), but Western States is the ultimate goal of many an ultra runner, and this might be the most comprehensive of all of them. A must-see.

Further Reading

80/20 RUNNING: RUN STRONGER AND RACE FASTER BY TRAINING SLOWER

MATT FITZGERALD (2014)

This is the book that finally helped me understand the training method of running slow to run fast. Glorious in its simplicity, Fitzgerald will go down as an all-timer running coach for this work.

BECOMING A SUSTAINABLE RUNNER: A GUIDE TO RUNNING FOR LIFE, COMMUNITY, AND PLANET

TINA MUIR AND ZOË ROM (2023)

A comprehensive three-step guide to developing your running practice in a way so that running can remain true to your personal values in the long run. Love how you run, who you run with and where you run.

BETTER, FASTER, FARTHER: HOW RUNNING CHANGED EVERYTHING WE KNOW ABOUT WOMEN

MAGGIE MERTENS (2024)

A brilliantly concise delivery of a long, long history of injustice against women framed within the world of running, contexualised against the rest of society.

BORN TO RUN: THE HIDDEN TRIBE, THE ULTRA-RUNNERS, AND THE GREATEST RACE THE WORLD HAS NEVER SEEN

CHRIS MCDOUGALL (2010)

It's the biggest-selling book about running for a reason. What a story! And it's grounded in deep research and wild lived experiences.

LIKE THE WIND – QUARTERLY MAGAZINE

If you own this book, you likely enjoy holding beautifully designed publications that are printed on heavyweight paper stock and filled with thoughtful, diverse stories. You'll also enjoy Like the Wind magazine.

THE LONGEST RACE: INSIDE THE SECRET WORLD OF ABUSE, DOPING, AND DECEPTION ON NIKE'S ELITE RUNNING TEAM

KARA GOUCHER (2023)

One of the most notorious memoir takedowns ever, two-time Olympian Goucher writes honestly about her time as a Nike athlete, and 'scandal' doesn't cover it.

RUNNING

LINDSEY A FREEMAN (2023)

This powder pink, pocket-sized collection of personal essays about a life spent running is maybe my favorite book about non-elite running. Written through an academic lens, using queer and feminist theory, it's a must-read.

RUNNING WHILE BLACK: FINDING FREEDOM IN A SPORT THAT WASN'T BUILT FOR US

ALISON M DESIR (2022)

If you understand that running is a political act, this book outlined every bit of that from a Black perspective at a crucial time. This book is about running, but anyone living in America can benefit from the stories told within.

RUNNING WITH THE KENYANS: PASSION, ADVENTURE, AND THE SECRETS OF THE FASTEST PEOPLE ON EARTH

ADHARANAND FINN (2010)

Finn, an excellent sports writer, uprooted his whole life (family and all) to move to Kenya to see if he could understand why excellence in running is so prevalent there. It makes you think about what's possible if you think about painting outside of the lines.

WHAT I TALK ABOUT WHEN I TALK ABOUT RUNNING

HARUKI MURAKAMI (2007)

One of the greatest living writers writes a memoir but it's centred around the art of long-distance running rather than writing? Fantastic. Inspirational. Filled with some absolutely perfect sentences.

Acknowledgements

My first book, eh? Published three and a bit years after a festive reunion with a schoolfriend I first met aged seven, but hadn't seen in 15 years. Thank you, Tom Tidyman, for the casual suggestion I try my hand at sports journalism. It all works out.

Without that seed of an idea, I never would've been able to work with the Batsford team, who always seemed to believe me when I told them I could meet their deadlines. Thanks so much to Rebecca Armstrong for commissioning and editing this book, Eoghan O'Brien and Russ Gilbert for making it look so beautiful, as well as James Kellow, Mia Autumn Roe and Peter Lee for helping it find its readers.

I would also never have met all the brilliant runners who have shared their stories with me, any of the runners (or not) who have read my work (or not), or, indeed, the many, many fellow running writers on Substack and beyond who have supplied so much daily creative inspiration and community connection. Your work is so important and valued.

Unreserved thanks to my excellent friends/editors James Ingram and Ben Perreau for the unbridled support in helping to shape and direct my ideas these past couple of years, and huge thanks to Lee Glandorf and Cole Bastedo for your timely, talented eyes on this manuscript.

Thanks to all my old friends who have told me that they now enjoy reading about running despite ... not running. Special thanks to Dan, Andrew and Mischa for being NYC-based inspiration at a crucial moment in the writing of this book, and to Chris, Dave, Hattie, Joe, Mau, and Tom for your important help and encouragement all along the way. Thanks as well to Rose and Mr Flynn for the writing desk that I'm sitting at right now.

Last, but certainly not least, thank you to my family. Thank you to my parents for never quite understanding what I do well enough to explain to their friends, but supporting me regardless, thank you to my children for being both the inspiration and hindrance to my every literary desire, and thank you to Stella. I never used that leather-bound book to take notes for my first book, but I promise the thought was there. You know that. You've read it all. I love you.

About the Author

Raziq Rauf is a running coach and journalist who uses a lifetime of experience and training as both a runner and as a writer to think a little more deeply about every possible aspect of the sport in his newsletter 'Running Sucks'.

He has previously written for the BBC, the Guardian, Classic Rock, and Kerrang! among others, contributing an in-depth look at nu metal in the 2013 anthology *The Art of Metal* towards the self-imposed end of his chapter as a music critic.

Born in London to Bangladeshi immigrant parents in 1983, he now lives in Los Angeles with his wife, two children, and his beautiful dog, Cindy.

WAY

Picture Credits

Page 2 © Dave Hashim; Page 5 © David Miller; Page 6 © Sean Haworth; Page 10 © Alamy / Associated Press / Masaaki Nakajima; Page 13 © Edgar García; Page 17 © Alamy / Associated Press / Elise Amendola; Page 18 © Sean Haworth; Page 25 © Dave Hashim; Page 26 © Dave Hashim; Page 29 © David Miller; Page 31 © Dave Hashim; Page 33 © Connor Simpson; Page 34 © Alamy / Xinhua; Page 36 © Alamy / 1Apix; Page 41 © Alamy / Andrew Summer; Page 43 © Alamy / Associated Press; Page 44 © Dave Hashim; Page 49 © David Miller; Page 51 © David Miller; Page 52–53 © David Miller; Page 55 © Alamy / ZUMA Press, Inc; Page 56 © Alamy / PA Images / Victoria Jones; Page 59 © Getty / ED JONES; Page 60 © Getty / pixdeluxe; Page 63 © Alamy / PA Images; Page 68–69 © Mark Hayes; Page 75 © Allie Bailey; Page 76 © Sean Haworth; Page 79 © Dave Hashim; Page 85 © Alamy / adsR; Page 86 © Dave Hashim; Page 89 © Alamy / dpa picture alliance; Page 91 © Laura Green; Page 92 © Alamy / Sueddeutsche Zeitung Photo / Johannes Simon; Page 95 © Getty / Pier Marco Tacca / Stringer; Page 97 © Alamy / Associated Press / Elise Amendola; Page 102 © Alamy / ZUMA Press, Inc.; Page 104 © Sean Haworth; Page 107 © Dave Hashim; Page 109 © Dave Hashim; Page 110 © Dave Hashim; Page 111 © Dave Hashim; Page 112 © Dave Hashim; Page 114–115 © Ed Cotton; Page 117 © Alamy / PCN Photography / Paul Sutton-PCN; Page 123 © Simon Roberts; Page 125 © Raziq Rauf; Page 126 © SOAR Running, photography by Lewis Greaves; Page 129 © SOAR Running, photography by Lewis Greaves; Page 130–131 © SOAR Running, photography by Lewis Greaves; Page 139 © Janji; Page 140–141 © PYNRS; Page 143 © Satisfy; Page 144 © Tracksmith; Page 148 © Alamy / sportpoint; Page 151 © Getty / Boston Globe; Page 153 © Dave Hashim; Page 157 © Alamy / Associated Press / Rich Pedroncelli; Page 158 © Alexis Berg; Page 162 © Ed Cotton; Page 165 © Sarah Ackland; Page 167 © Jessica Zapotechne; Page 168 © Alamy / Imago / Juliane Sonntag; Page 171 © Getty / Patrick Fraser; Page 172 © Steve Rapport; Page 173 © Steve Rapport; Page 176 © Sean Haworth; Page 180 © Edgar García; Page 181 © Edgar García; Page 185 © Dylan Harris; Page 186 © Dylan Harris; Page 187 © Dylan Harris; Page 192 © Dave Hashim; Page 193 © Dave Hashim; Page 196 © Alamy / Mika Volkmann; Page 199 © Alamy / Steve Krull Running Images; Page 200–201 © David Miller; Page 203 © Alamy / ZUMA Press Inc.; Page 208 Ultra-Trail Ninghai; Page 209 © Ryan Thrower; Page 212 © Sean Haworth; Page 216–217 © David Miller; Page 220 © Alamy / Sipa US; Page 222 © Alamy / Godong; Page 234 © Dave Hashim.

All reasonable efforts have been taken to ensure that the reproduction of the content in this book is done with the full consent of the copyright owners. If you are aware of unintentional omissions, please contact the company directly so that any necessary corrections may be made for future editions.

Sources

© Henry Miller, *Stand Still Like the Hummingbird*, New Directions Publishing (1962)

Haruki Murakami, What I Talk About When I Talk About Running, Vintage (2009)

OPPOSITE

Runners take part in the NYCRUNS Cocoa Classic 5K and 10K.

Index

First published in the United Kingdom in 2026 by

Batsford
43 Great Ormond Street
London
WC1N 3HZ

An imprint of B. T. Batsford Holdings Limited

Copyright © B. T. Batsford Ltd 2026
Text copyright © Raziq Rauf 2026

All rights reserved. No part of this publication may be copied, displayed, extracted, reproduced, utilized, stored in a retrieval system or transmitted in any form or by any means, electronic, mechanical or otherwise including but not limited to photocopying, recording, or scanning without the prior written permission of the publishers.

ISBN 9781837330423

A CIP catalogue record for this book is available from the British Library.

10 9 8 7 6 5 4 3 2 1

Reproduction by Rival Colour Ltd, UK
Printed by Dream Colour, China

This book can be ordered direct from the publisher at www.batsfordbooks.com, or try your local bookshop

Distributed throughout the UK and Europe by Abrams & Chronicle Books, 1st Floor, 22–24 Ely Place, London EC1N 6TE and 57 rue Gaston Tessier, 75166 Paris, France

www.abramsandchronicle.co.uk
info@abramsandchronicle.co.uk